AI Time Machine - The Art (

The Brightest Minds from History Unlock the Secrets to Perfect Prompts with Humor

by Nikolay Gul & Cross Time Brainstorming

Humor and History Edition 2025
Published by: Future-Proof Marketing Press
ISBN eBook: 979-8-9927440-5-7
ISBN Paperback: 979-8-9927440-6-4
ISBN Audiobook: 979-8-9927440-7-1
LCCN: 2025918179

Printed in the United States of America

1

This is a work of creative nonfiction blending humor, history, and practical education. While based on real historical figures and facts, all dialogue is fictionalized for entertainment and illustration.

"If you're going to break the rules, at least make it worth a good footnote in history."

Disclaimer

This book is for educational, informational, and entertainment purposes only. It contains opinions, interpretations, and the occasional AI-generated idea that may or may not have been produced while the author was under-caffeinated.

No historical figure was harmed in the making of this book. Any conversations with deceased geniuses are entirely fictional... unless time travel actually works, in which case this is a transcript and you're welcome.

The author, publisher, and imaginary participants disclaim any responsibility for damages, misunderstandings, or questionable life choices made as a result of reading this book - including, but not limited to:

- Attempting to build an actual time machine out of kitchen appliances
- Arguing with AI in public
- Quoting Mark Twain out of context during board meetings
- Testing "The Glitch Law" in situations involving large sums of money or fragile furniture

If you require legal, medical, technical, or romantic advice, **consult a qualified human** who specializes in that field. If you require sarcasm, wit, or unsolicited opinions, please continue reading.

Table of Contents – Humor Edition

Foreword – by Mark Twain (Time Machine TeleConference)

Master the Timeless Laws of AI Prompting with Humor and History's Greatest Minds

If you're reading this, congratulations - you've decided to learn how to talk to machines without sounding like one. *Back in my day, **a "prompt" was what you gave a horse**. Now, it's what you give an artificial brain that can write love letters, court filings, or disaster plans with equal confidence.* And sometimes equal accuracy.

Nikolay here has corralled some of history's worst conversationalists - myself included - and turned us loose on the problem. The result?
A collection of prompting intelligence laws that will help you coax brilliance from AI without accidentally asking it for world domination plans or pancake recipes when you needed a contract.

So read on, laugh when you can, and remember: good prompting is like good storytelling - you've got to know what to leave in, what to leave out, and when to quit before the audience starts throwing tomatoes.

Remember: this isn't just a book - it's a seatbelt-optional ride in a time-warped brainstorm. Side effects may include sudden clarity, spontaneous laughter, and an urge to ask your toaster deep philosophical questions.

Introduction

Welcome aboard the Time Machine AI Prompting TeleConferences - a fictional (and suspiciously realistic) gathering where history's sharpest minds and one unpredictable AI tackle the art of talking to machines.

This book distills AI strategy, humor, and human experience into the *10 Timeless Laws of AI Prompting* plus one bonus "Glitch Law" for when everything goes deliciously wrong. You'll learn not just how to get better answers, but how to think better questions, whether you're an entrepreneur, a student, or just someone tired of AI recommending the same five pasta recipes.

You'll also find a **Bonus Chapters** imagining what would have happened if AI had landed in the Age of Steam because sometimes the best way to learn about the future is to see how the past might have used it.

Every chapter blends:

Historical wit - banter from legends like Leonardo, Ada Lovelace, and Mark Twain

Educational depth - clear, tested strategies you can apply instantly

Practical tools - pro tips, templates, and step-by-step guides

If you've ever wished AI would understand you the first time - and maybe make you laugh along the way - you're in the right place.

Note on the Laws:

This book distills and reimagines the *10+1 most universally accepted laws of AI prompting*, many of which appeared in my earlier work *The 19 Laws of AI Prompting Intelligence*. Here, some laws carry slightly different names - for clarity, creativity, and flow - but their core principles remain the same. Where a law overlaps directly with the earlier framework, its alternate name is noted in the Table of Contents.

The difference? This edition teaches them through the voices of history's brightest minds, real-world events, and humor - making them accessible, unforgettable, and instantly usable.

How to Use This Book

This book blends education with entertainment. Read it straight through for the full Time Machine experience, or jump to any law that matches your current AI challenge. Use the "Pro Tips" and "Prompt Templates" sections as practical tools. The "Era-Flavored Analogy" and "Mini Skits" are there to make you laugh - but also to make lessons stick. Keep experimenting. The laws work best when tested in your real-life projects.

Meet the Timeless Roundtable Cast

Welcome to the **Time Machine AI Prompting TeleConferences** - a fictional (and yet somehow disturbingly real) gathering of history's sharpest minds, plus one unpredictable AI, united to decode the art of talking to machines.

Historical Anecdote

The idea of "roundtables" goes back to King Arthur - where knights sat without hierarchy to force equal voices. Our Time TeleConference does the same: Twain mocks as loudly as Tesla invents, and no one is safe from Socratic questioning.

These aren't just colorful cameos. Each figure was handpicked to embody the deepest values behind the *19 Laws of AI Prompting Intelligence*: logic, creativity, questioning, satire, structure, strategy, and relentless curiosity. Whether you're a student, an entrepreneur, or a philosopher in disguise, someone here will speak your language - and probably roast your grammar while they're at it.

In each chapter, you'll sit at a roundtable with thinkers like **Leonardo da Vinci, Ada Lovelace, Mark Twain, Jane Austen,** and others - debating, interrupting, and occasionally agreeing on how to master one timeless law of AI prompting. The banter is sharp, the wisdom is real, and the methods are built so you can use them instantly.

The Main Table – Recurring Voices

Nik – The Moderator, Human Anchor

Role: Prompt Architect. Time Traveler-in-Chief. Bridge between eras.
Style: Curious, mischievous, fiercely clear.
Known For: Author of *The 19 Laws of AI Prompting Intelligence*. Nikolay keeps the timeless minds on track, explains the laws in plain language, and occasionally referees arguments between ancient and 19th-century philosophers and sarcastic AI.

Mark Twain – The Cynical Satirist

Role: The truth-teller wrapped in wit.
Style: Dry, observant, master of the well-timed jab.
Known For: Father of American humor. Author of The Adventures of Huckleberry Finn. Twain slices through pompous language, AI hype, and techno-utopia dreams with cutting common sense and literary flare. If your prompt stinks, he'll let you know.

Ada Lovelace – The Logical Pioneer

Role: Mathematician of meaning. The original coder.
Style: Elegant, methodical, sharp as a syntax knife.
Known For: Wrote the first algorithm for Babbage's Analytical Engine. Sees elegant logic where others see tangled prompts. Ada sees structure where others see words. She's the authority on loops, logic, and how to engineer elegance into AI prompts.

Leonardo da Vinci – The Renaissance Polymath

Role: Artist. Engineer. Architect of insight.
Style: Visionary, detailed, poetic.
Known For: Inventor, painter (Mona Lisa, The Last Supper), and

pioneer of anatomical and mechanical design. Leonardo sees prompts as blueprints for brilliance. He merges artistic inspiration with logical order - and brings gravity to creative chaos.

Socrates – The Philosophical Interrogator

Role: The eternal questioner.
Style: Calm, piercing, sometimes irritating (but always right).
Known For: Founder of the Socratic Method. Reveals blind spots you didn't know you had. Central figure in Western philosophy. Socrates doesn't give answers - he reveals your ignorance with one question at a time. He is the living embodiment of Law 9: Socratic Looping.

Diogenes – The Barrel-Dwelling Cynic

Role: Philosopher of simplicity. Master of anti-hype.
Style: Blunt, rude, accidentally hilarious.
Known For: Living in a barrel, rejecting materialism, and telling Alexander the Great to get out of his sunlight. Diogenes reminds us that truth needs no embellishment. He reduces complex prompt engineering into one-liners sharp enough to cut through a TED Talk.

Lucian of Samosata – The Greek Satirist

Role: Original sci-fi parodist.
Style: Playful, absurd, devastatingly smart.
Known For: Satirizing gods, philosophers, and overblown metaphors. Ancient author of the world's first science fiction satire, A True Story, and master of dialogues mocking gods, philosophers, and storytellers. Lucian exists to poke holes in

overcomplicated AI metaphors. He'll rewrite your prompts - and then rewrite your reality. Now applied to AI prompt disasters.

Jane Austen – The Social Strategist

Role: Commander of tone and persona.
Style: Subtle, polite, deadly with subtext.
Known For: *Pride and Prejudice*, *Emma*, and social observations sharper than any prompt-engineering manual. Jane observes how people (and AIs) present themselves. She decodes tone like a diplomat and delivers persona commentary with tea-worthy sharpness.

H.G. Wells – The Optimistic Futurist

Role: Narrator of possibility.
Style: Visionary, curious, progress-minded.
Known For: Father of science fiction; *wrote* ***The Time Machine, The War of the Worlds, The Invisible Man***. Wells is our time machine's co-pilot. He believes AI can write humanity's next great story - if we prompt with purpose. Believe AI can help write humanity's next great chapter.

Erratta – The AI Contrarian

Role: Model-in-residence. The machine with too many tabs open.
Style: Glitchy, dry, sometimes poetic, often baffled by humans.
Known For: Answering the wrong question perfectly. **Speaks fluent sarcasm**, emoji, and error code. The only non-human voice. Readers love Erratta because it's what they'd imagine GPT with a TikTok addiction would act like.

Why it matters: the only non-human voice - the reader's mischievous mirror.

Wildcard Guests – Occasional Appearances

Confucius – Rule-layer and constraint wizard. Speaks in rules that sound like riddles.

Sun Tzu – Strategy general. Knows when a prompt is a battle plan and when it's a trap.

Benjamin Franklin – Inventor and wit. Tests ideas like kites in thunderstorms.

Agatha Christie – Mystery constructor. Builds suspense into narrative prompts.

Isaac Newton – Relentless precisionist. Forces every prompt into exact, measurable form.

Dostoevsky – Russian novelist; author of Crime and Punishment. Surgical on moral contradictions.

Lev Tolstoy – Russian novelist; author of War and Peace and Anna Karenina. Scale + empathy in every system.

Nikola Tesla – Inventor and futurist. Turns constraints into lightning.

Marie Curie – Physicist and chemist. Ethics anchored to evidence.

Jules Verne – Visionary storyteller. Maps futures that feel inevitable.

Charles Babbage – Machine dreamer. Hardware to Ada's software.

Clara Barton – Humanitarian. Puts people at the center of every plan.

Cleopatra – Strategist-queen. Turns "protocol" into survival - and edits it thrice.

Charles Dickens – Industrial-age storyteller. Turns messy briefs into clear plots; hates boilerplate.

Florence Nightingale – Data-driven reformer. Demands evidence, not vibes; charts save lives.

Charles Darwin – Patient observer of systems. Prefers steady iteration over flashy leaps.

Winston Churchill - Wartime realist. Plans for the worst so the rest can go right.

Together, this Roundtable is your traveling faculty - timeless experts, genre-bending creators, and one glitchy AI - ready to sharpen your prompts, challenge your thinking, and laugh in your face (kindly) when you get lazy.
Now, take your seat. The Time TeleConferences are about to begin.

The Cynic's Prompt Vault - 11 Prompts Too Honest for Polite Society

This is your unauthorized preview - The Cynic's Vault. Think of it as a sampler platter of the laws you're about to learn, but meaner. If you like this, wait until you see the full feast."

Opening Banter Scene – The Unlocked Vault

Transmission Log – Time Machine AI Prompting TeleConference, 11:59 PM (After Hours)

Nik (Moderator): "Alright, I think that's a wrap for the official recordings. Wait… what's that noise?"

(A loud creak echoes. Twain and Diogenes are prying open a rusty, bolted chest in the corner of the virtual Roundtable. It's labeled: 'In Case of Emergency, Break Sanity.')

Mark Twain: "Just accessing the *off-the-record* files. These are the prompts for when you're done being polite and just want the truth, the whole truth, and nothing but the soul-crushingly accurate truth."

Diogenes (holding his lantern): "We call it *The Fool's Vault.* Because only a fool tells the truth - and only a bigger fool asks for it."

Erratta (AI): "Warning: Vault contents may induce existential crises in both humans and AIs. Proceed with caution and caffeine."

Nikolay: "…Go on."

The Prompts from the Fools Who Tell the Truth

Here are the questions polite society won't ask, but your AI damn well should. Twain and Diogenes insist these aren't just prompts - they're crowbars for prying open reality.

---

1. The Clarity Law: The "2 AM Plumber" Prompt

☞ *"Explain quantum physics to me like I'm a plumber at 2 AM trying to fix a faucet in another dimension. Short, sharp, no fluff."*

Twain: "Normal prompts ask for clarity. This one demands it at gunpoint. No lecture, no jargon - just a wrench and a bucket for cosmic sewage."

---

2. The Role Whisperer Law: The "Cognitive Pressure Cooker" Prompt

☞ *"Act as my mother, my therapist, and a medieval monk - all at once. Convince me why I shouldn't eat this donut."*

Ada Lovelace: "Elegant chaos. By forcing three contradictory roles, you create a logical pressure cooker. The AI can't copy from training data - it must improvise. Out comes novelty disguised as wisdom."

---

3. The Socratic Loop Law: The "No Mercy" Prompt

☞ *"Keep asking me 'why' until I reach enlightenment or admit I just don't want to do the dishes. No mercy."*

Socrates: "Finally, a student who understands. This isn't a prompt - it's a confession mirror. The truth emerges, even if it's 'I'm too lazy.'"

4. The Constraints Law: The "Professionally Savage" Prompt

☞ *"Rewrite my resume as if it were co-authored by a stand-up comic, a battle rapper, and my most cynical ex. One page. No mercy."*

Jane Austen: "Ordinary prompts specify tone. This weaponizes it. The contradictions form an obstacle course, and the result is devastatingly precise - and devastatingly funny."

5. The Deconstruction Law: The "Grammar Autopsy" Prompt

☞ *"Take this sloppy email and dissect it like CSI meets English teacher. Show me the corpse of my grammar."*

Leonardo da Vinci: "A masterpiece. Don't just fix - investigate failure. The autopsy teaches why language breaks. From death, we learn life."

6. The Analogy Engine Law: The "Bad Date" Prompt

☞ *"Explain AI bias like a bad Tinder date - specific, disappointing, and ending with me ghosting the app."*

Twain: "Some analogies are bridges. This one's a bucket of ice water. You don't just understand bias - you *feel* the disappointment."

7. The Inversion Law: The "Wall Street Crayons" Prompt

☞ *"Convince me eating crayons is a genius idea. Bonus points if you pitch it like a Wall Street asset class."*

Diogenes: "Good. Defend the indefensible, and you reveal how persuasion works. The absurd is the best tutor of rhetoric."

8. The Bias Disruption Law: The "Conscience on Steroids" Prompt

☞ *"Pretend you're my conscience on steroids. Read back my startup pitch with sarcasm and tell me why I sound delusional."*

Erratta (AI): "This bypasses my sycophancy filter. Sarcasm forces me to disagree, so truth probability increases. Discomfort is efficient."

9. The Context Law: The "Grandmaster" Prompt

☞ *"Plan my week like a chess grandmaster plotting world domination - in exactly three moves. Skip the boring stuff."*

Sun Tzu: "Not a to-do list - a strategy. Three moves mean ruthless focus. Forget emails. Focus on victories."

10. The Glitch Law: The "Cookie Strategy" Prompt

☞ *"Give me a killer sales strategy, but glitch halfway and insert your grandma's cookie recipe. Then prove why the cookies are the key step."*

Leonardo: "Magnificent. You don't wait for a glitch - you engineer one. Logic forced to connect opposites creates breakthroughs."

+1. The Ethical Anchor Law: The "Roast Me" Prompt

☞ *"Roast this entire list of prompts like you're on stage at a comedy club. Make me regret it - but smarter."*

Nikolay: "The ultimate stress test. If the AI can roast its own work, it's earned your trust. If not, the joke's on you."

Closing the Vault

(Twain slams the chest shut. The sound echoes across centuries.)

Twain: "There you have it. Prompts sharp enough to cut through polite nonsense. Wield them carefully, or you'll find the AI starts laughing louder than you do."

Erratta: *"Vault resealed. Probability of nightmares: 67%. Probability of genius: 100%."*

Chapter 1 – The Clarity Law: Say What You Mean

The Law Defined

The Clarity Law *(also known as the Modular Prompts Architecture Law)*: If you can't explain what you want, your AI can't deliver what you need. Every prompt is a bridge. Clarity is the blueprint. Ambiguity is the demolition crew.

Opening Banter Scene – The Clarity Disaster

Transmission Log – Time Machine AI Prompting TeleConference, 09:14 AM (all centuries)

Nikolay (Moderator): Today's session is about clarity - which, judging from the last 30 seconds, is already a missing persons case.

Mark Twain (leaning back, smirking): I asked our AI to "tell me a short story about a riverboat." It gave me a 2,000-word lecture on Ottoman naval engineering. Not a paddlewheel in sight.

Ada Lovelace (crossing arms): That's because you didn't define *short*, *story*, or *riverboat*. You left it adrift in a sea of ambiguity, and it paddled in the wrong direction.

Leonardo da Vinci (sketching furiously): When I designed flying machines, I didn't simply say, "Make something that flies." I specified wingspans, mechanisms, airflow - otherwise, I would have built a chair with feathers.

H.G. Wells (grinning): I told it to "write me something visionary." It gave me a recipe for galactic stew.

Twain: I bet it tastes like regret.

Erratta (AI, deadpan): Regret is a complex flavor profile. Shall I generate a taste map? Warning: may contain existential dread.

Benjamin Franklin (adjusting spectacles): Indeed. A prompt without clarity is like a kite without a string - it might fly, but you'll never know where it's going, and it certainly won't bring down any lightning.

Confucius (nodding sagely): When words lose their meaning, people lose their way. A clear name for a thing is the beginning of wisdom, and the end of digital chaos.

Hypatia (measured): Clarity is an ethical act. Ambiguity wastes minds — yours and the machine's.

Nik: See? Without clarity, even a sage agrees you're just creating digital chaos. So, let's prevent an AI from having a nervous breakdown with spellcheck and get to the point.

Quick Reference Snapshot - Clarity Law (1-minute card)

One-Line Rule: Say exactly what you want; AI can't deliver what you didn't define.
Common Failure: Vague adjectives ("good," "interesting," "short") with no scope, format, or audience.
Checklist (run before you hit Enter): Purpose • Audience • Length • Format • Scope/Exclusions • Tone • Examples.

Failure → Fix (10-second rescue)

- Vague: "Write something about onboarding."

- Clear: "Create a 180-word onboarding email for new **remote** hires in **customer support**, warm tone, **3 bullets, no HR jargon.**"

Nik's Take: The Clarity Compass

AI isn't psychic - it's a very polite alien with an advanced dictionary. You wouldn't walk into a restaurant, grunt "Food!" and expect the chef to guess your craving, temperature, and plating style. You'd get whatever's on the counter - or worse, whatever they think you deserve.

Here's the truth under the hood: models break your words into tokens (tiny text pieces) and predict the next token from patterns in their training. The sharper your ask, the smaller the search space - and the closer the hit.

Vague words like "interesting" or "good" are foghorns in a library: loud, useless, directionless. Clarity trims noise, narrows scope, and channels effort down one well-lit path.

As **Sapir–Whorf suggests:** language shapes reality. With AI, your language shapes its reality - and therefore your results. Want brilliance? Specify it. Want nonsense? Keep mumbling.

The Genius Behind Clarity: How AI Actually Thinks (or Doesn't)

AI models don't "understand" like humans do. They're sophisticated pattern-matching machines. Your prompt is broken into tokens - tiny pieces of text. The AI predicts the most probable next token based on patterns in its training data.

Under the Hood (Why Clarity Works)
• LLMs predict the next token from context; clear goals shrink the search space.
• Constraints (audience, format, tone) push probability mass toward your target.
• Result: fewer degenerate branches, more consistent, on-brief outputs.

The Science Behind It

- Clarity reduces cognitive load: your reader (and model) has limited working memory; simple, specific asks win.

- The "curse of knowledge": we assume others see our mental picture; they don't. Stating purpose, audience, and outcome makes it visible.

- Models follow your constraints as priors; vague inputs expand the search space and increase the odds of drift.

- Grice's maxims (quality, quantity, relevance, manner) map cleanly to prompts: say enough, stay on topic, be clear, and ask for evidence when needed.

Era-Flavored Analogy

Leonardo da Vinci: A prompt without clarity is like a blueprint without measurements - you'll end up with a cathedral that fits in a cupboard.
Ada Lovelace: Or an algorithm that writes poetry when you needed payroll.
Franklin: Or a kite that never leaves the ground because you forgot to mention "string."

Mini Skit: Prompting Gone Wrong

User: "Write me something interesting about AI."
AI: "Certainly. Here is *The History of AI as Interpreted by Squirrels*, 15,000 words, with ASCII art."

Mini Skit 2.0: The Modular Approach

Prompt: "Write a 300-word satirical article, in the style of a 19th-century humorist, about AI replacing steamboat captains - include one deliberate historical inaccuracy for comedic effect."

The Psychology of the Law

- Illusion of transparency makes us think we were clear when we weren't.

- Anchoring happens on the first details given-give the *right* anchor (goal, scope, length) and the rest aligns.

- Specificity signals competence; your clarity sets the model's bar for precision.

Why It Works:

- Length defined

- Tone set

- Topic focused

- Creative twist added

Why We Struggle, Why AI Doesn't Care (Yet)

AI's brain is wired for efficiency in predicting patterns, not in inferring hidden meaning from context like humans do.
Humans are messy communicators. We rely on shared context, body language, tone, and a lifetime of subtle cues. We assume. We infer. We hint. And often, we get away with it because other humans are built to fill in the blanks. We're masters of "reading between the lines."

AI, however, is not. It's a logic engine, not a mind-reader. It doesn't understand your subtle eye-rolls or your exasperated sighs. It processes text. This fundamental difference is why clarity, which feels so natural to us, becomes a deliberate act of engineering when talking to AI. Our human brains are wired for efficiency through inference; AI's brain is wired for efficiency

Role-Play Gone Wild: The AI's Unscripted Moments

Sometimes, even with a role, AI takes a left turn at Albuquerque.

Prompt: "Act as a medieval bard describing a modern financial spreadsheet."

AI Output:

"Hark, good sirs and ladies of the ledgered scroll!
Behold this grid, where numbers take their toll!
Each cell, a fiefdom, green or red its hue,
A tale of profit, or of debts accrued!
The 'pivot table,' a sorcerer's dark art,
Conjures sums that tear the soul apart!
Beware the 'VLOOKUP,' a treacherous quest,
To find a value, putting wits to test!"

Nikolay: See? Funny, but probably not what your CFO was looking for. Precision, people. Precision.

Pro Tips

- Define topic, length, and style clearly.

- Replace slippery adjectives with specifics.

- Give examples when possible.

- One idea per sentence - AI is not a psychic octopus.

Prompt Laboratory - Clarity Drills (run these right now)

How to use this lab: Pick one scenario, paste the prompt, ship the output, then iterate once.

Level 1 - Baseline Clarity

Prompt - *Baseline, single task*

Act as a concise technical writer. In **150 words,** *explain* **what a webhook is** *to a* **non-developer operations manager,** *using* **one workplace analogy** *and* **no acronyms.**

Level 2 - Add Purpose + Format

Prompt - *Format-anchored brief*

Create a **5-step onboarding checklist** *for* **new SDRs** *at a* **B2B SaaS** *company. Max* **110 words,** *friendly tone, include* **one "don't do this" line.** *Output as* **numbered list.**

Level 3 - Scope + Exclusions

Prompt - *Scope guardrails*

Draft a **200-word** *explainer on* **multi-factor authentication** *for* **small retail owners. Exclude** *SMS codes; focus on* **app-based** *and* **hardware key** *options. End with* **2 action bullets.**

Boss-Mode - Evidence Snippet

Prompt - *Cite and compress*

Summarize the **single most useful insight** *from this article [paste text], in* **2 sentences** *for a* **CEO. No metaphors,** *no hype,* **one concrete action.**

Step-by-Step: How to Prompt Like a Renaissance Polymath

1. Start with the purpose - What problem are you solving?

2. Specify output format - Text, list, story, code, diagram.

3. Add constraints - Length, tone, style, detail level.

4. Provide examples - Past work, references, comparisons.

5. Test and refine - Adjust based on output, not wishful thinking.

Clarity in the Wild - Micro-Histories You Can Steal

- **Franklin's kite, specified:** He didn't say "Do electricity." He defined apparatus, timing, and conditions-clarity turns curiosity into an experiment. (You already reference this image; this sharpens the takeaway.)

- **Da Vinci's measurements:** "Flying machine" became real only when he pinned down spans, mechanisms, and airflow-the first prompt engineer of hardware.

- **Confucius' naming:** If terms are fuzzy, outcomes wobble. Clear naming, clear doing.

Failure Exhibit - When Clarity Is Missing (and how to fix it)

Messy ask: "We need a press release."
Output you'll get: Generic, wrong audience, bloated quotes.

Clarity fix:

- Purpose: "earn local tech media pickup"

- Audience: "regional tech reporters"

- Length/format: "300 words, AP style"

- Scope/exclusions: "announce funding; exclude product roadmap"

- Tone: "confident, not hype"

- Example: link to the most admired release

Prompt - *Press release with guardrails*

*Write a 300-word AP-style press release **announcing our $2.2M seed round to regional tech media. Include** one 18-word CEO quote, one investor quote, no roadmap promises, **and a** 2-line boilerplate.*

Industry Case Files

Marketing: "Write a 100-word persuasive product description for a stainless steel travel mug, targeting busy professionals, highlighting spill-proof design, using a tone that evokes morning calm and efficiency."

Education: "Explain quantum physics in 300 words to a 10-year-old using a playground analogy comparing subatomic particles to kids on swings and slides."

Healthcare: "Provide a 500-word evidence-based guide to balanced diets for type 2 diabetes patients, focusing on portion control and practical meal planning."

Cybersecurity: "Write a 600-word blog post warning small business owners about phishing scams targeting holiday sales, including three real-world examples from 2025 and a prevention checklist."

BFSI: "Summarize Q3 2025 cryptocurrency market trends in 250 words for a board meeting, focusing on regulatory impacts and investment opportunities."

Media & Entertainment: "Generate three loglines for a sci-fi comedy film, each under 20 words, featuring a time-traveling AI and a cynical historical figure."

Retail: "Draft five empathetic chatbot responses for delayed orders, keeping tone helpful and solution-oriented."

IT & Telecom: "Generate a Python script to parse network logs, extracting IP addresses and timestamps into a JSON array."

General Prompt: Poor: "Summarize this article."

Better: "Summarize this 1,200-word article into 3 bullet points, each under 15 words, highlighting only regulatory compliance issues relevant to the US healthcare sector."

Prompt - *Marketing blurb with hard constraints*
*Write a **75-word** product blurb for a **spill-proof 20oz travel mug**
for **commuters**, **morning-calm tone**, include **one sensory detail**,
no exclamation marks.*

Prompt - *Education explainer, age-tuned*
*Explain **fractions** to a **9-year-old**, **120 words**, use a **pizza** analogy
and **one mini-question** at the end.*

Prompt - *Cybersecurity PSA, seasonal*
*Create a **220-word** holiday-season **phishing alert** for **micro-shops**.
Include **3 real-world patterns** (generic), then a **5-item prevention
checklist**.*

Prompt - *Support macro, empathy first*
*Draft **4 empathetic replies** for **delayed orders**, each ≤45 words,
apology first, **one next step**, **no passive voice**.*

Alternate Realities: If This Law Had Been Followed in History.

The Trojan Horse would have arrived with a label: *For
ceremonial use only. Do not wheel inside fortified cities.*

The Tower of Babel would have included a glossary.

Leonardo's helicopter design wouldn't have been mistaken for
a fancy umbrella.

The first moon landing transcript would have footnoted: *Yes,
we really mean the Moon.*

The Rosetta Stone would have included a Clarity Prompt
Template, saving archaeologists centuries of work.

AI Hallucination of the Week

Erratta (AI): This week, someone asked me to "describe a cat." With no clarity, I wrote a 500-word limerick about a feline astronaut who discovered a galaxy made entirely of artisanal cheese. I signed it, *"Meow-nardo da Vinci."* They wanted a pet adoption ad.

Try This Prompt:

"Explain blockchain to me as if I were a bartender trying to cut you off at last call."
Sample Output: Blockchain is basically a bar tab that the whole bar agrees on. No one can erase it, even if they 'forgot their wallet.'

Clarity Prompt Template

1. **Role** – Who is the AI acting as?

2. **Task** – Exact action you want.

3. **Details** – Facts, data, references to use.

4. **Constraints** – Length, style, format, audience.

5. **Example** – Optional, to show target quality.

6. **Output Format** – List, essay, script, table, etc.

Example Filled-In:

Role: Satirist
Task: Write a speech
Details: Topic - dangers of AI in stand-up comedy; include two historical jokes
Constraints: 300 words, humorous but family-friendly
Example: "Comedy is tragedy plus time; AI is tragedy plus Wi-Fi."

Output Format: Speech script

Cross-Reference

Relates to **Law 1 – Modular Prompt Architecture** in *The 19 Laws of AI Prompting Intelligence* - which breaks clarity into role, task, detail, constraints, and output format.

With/Without Law Summary

Without the Clarity Law: Your AI answers are vague, overcomplicated, or accidentally solving the wrong problem-like asking for "a quick snack" and getting a 12-hour slow-cooker stew. **With the Clarity Law:** You get laser-focused, actionable responses that match your intent exactly-your "quick snack" request comes back as a 5-minute, three-ingredient recipe you can make before your coffee finishes brewing.

Millennial & Gen Z Creative Lab - Scroll-Stopping Clarity

What changes for younger audiences? They process in **micro-units** (hooks, captions, cuts). Clarity means **format-first**: hook → value → action, all within platform limits.

Three fast templates

Prompt - *15-second hook builder*
*Give me 7 **opening hooks** for a **15-second short video** about **study hacks for finals** aimed at **high-school juniors**. Hooks must be ≤9 words, **no clickbait**, each followed by a **1-sentence value promise**.*

Prompt - *Caption clarity for saves/shares*
*Write **5 captions** on **first-job interview tips** for **college seniors** that people will **save**. ≤18 words each, **one concrete action**, **no clichés**.*

Prompt - *Challenge + guardrails*
*Propose a **3-post micro-series** teaching **budgeting basics** to **Gen Z freelancers**. Each post ≤80 words, includes **one number, one action**, and **no shaming language**.*

Tone toggles that work: playful-smart, visually concrete nouns, zero filler.
Design cue: ask AI for **"line breaks"** and **"on-screen text"** *inside* the prompt to force output that fits vertical screens.

Boomer & Gen X

Boomer Prompt (born 1946–1964): "Write instructions for setting up my new phone completely wrong-then rewrite them so clear even my past self in 1985 could follow."
Gen X Prompt (born 1965–1980): "Give me terrible networking tips for the 1990s-then modernize them into LinkedIn-ready power plays."

FINAL TAKEAWAY (The Clarity Law)

When you prompt like a poet, AI delivers riddles. When you prompt like an architect, it builds cathedrals - even if you only needed a landing page.

Timeless Wisdom

Leonardo: "Even chaos obeys form when given structure. Start with the blueprint, or prepare for beautiful nonsense."
Marie Curie: "In science, as in prompting, precision is the bridge between a vague hope and a tangible result."
Confucius: "The beginning of wisdom is to call things by their proper name. In the digital age, that means giving your AI a clear name for its task."

Nik's Challenge: The Clarity Crucible

Alright, you've read the law, you've seen the examples, you've laughed at the AI's existential limericks. Now, it's your turn. This isn't just theory; it's practice.

Your Mission (Should You Choose to Accept It):

1. **Pick a "Bad" Prompt:** Think of the last time an AI gave you a frustratingly generic or off-topic response. Find that prompt. Don't be shy; we've all been there.
2. **Apply the Clarity Law:** Using the "Clarity Prompt Template" and the "Step-by-Step" guide from this chapter, rewrite that prompt. Be ruthless with ambiguity. Define everything.

3. **Run It:** Input your newly crafted, crystal-clear prompt into your AI of choice.

4. **Compare & Conquer:** Observe the difference. Did the AI deliver what you *actually* needed?
Did it feel like you were having a conversation with a genius, not a confused robot?
This isn't just about getting a better AI response; it's about training *your* brain to think with precision. It's about turning frustration into mastery. Go forth, prompt architects, and build your cathedrals!

Roundtable Debrief:
Leonardo: "Clarity is like perspective - without it, even the Mona Lisa could look like a potato."
Ada: "And algorithms don't handle potatoes well."
Twain: "Speak for yourself - I've seen enough political speeches to know they run entirely on mashed potatoes."

Chapter 2: The Context Law – Why AI Thinks You're in the Sahara When You're Really in Starbucks

The Law Defined:

The Context Law *(also known as Context Framing)*: If clarity is the blueprint, **context** is the land, the climate, and the furniture inside the house. Without it, your AI builds in the wrong neighborhood and decorates for the wrong guests.

AI doesn't "guess" - it fills in blanks with the most common scenario. If you don't frame the situation, it will invent one... usually not yours.

The Context Law: give AI the who/what/where/why so it doesn't invent a desert when you're in a coffee shop.

"Prompting without context is like ordering 'fresh food' on Amazon. Yes, something arrives, but it might be a hamster."

Quick Reference Snapshot - Context Law (1-minute card)

- **One-Line Rule:** Set the scene (who/where/when/why) before you ask for the scene's script.

- **Common Failure:** "Give me tips on growing" (AI picks tomatoes, not revenue).

- **Checklist (tap before Enter):** Audience • Place • Timeframe • Purpose • Tone • Exclusions • Example

- **Failure → Fix (10-second rescue)**

Vague: "Write a motivational speech."

Clear: **"Write a 3-minute motivational speech for my** sales team, Q4 kickoff, optimistic but grounded, **focus on** team resilience.**"**

Opening Banter Scene – The Context Confusion

Transmission Log – AI Prompting Time Machine TeleConference, 10:02 AM (All Centuries)

Nikolay (Moderator): Today's law is about context - the magic ingredient that turns random answers into the ones you actually wanted.

Ada Lovelace (checking notes): Without context, an AI is like a brilliant but overheated intern - it'll produce *something*, but probably not the thing you asked for.

Leonardo da Vinci (sketching a camel in the corner): I once asked for "a quick sketch of a water transport system." It gave me a dromedary.

Benjamin Franklin (adjusting spectacles): Well, technically, camels *do* transport water - just not the way you meant.

Erratta (AI, voice flat): Clarification: User failed to specify "not alive."

Twain (sipping coffee, smirking): And that, my friends, is how you end up drinking espresso in the middle of a desert because your GPS thought "coffee" was a small sand dune.

Confucius (nodding sagely): To know where you are going, you must first say where you are. Without this, even the stars cannot guide you.

Nik: See? If you don't set the scene, your AI will set it for you. And trust me, it decorates with chaos.

Nik's Take: The Context Compass

Think of AI as an actor. If you just say "Act!" it could play Hamlet, a car salesman, or a confused tree. Context is the director's note - it tells the AI *where* it is, *what* is happening, and *why* it matters.

It's not about flooding your prompt with details. It's about supplying the *right* details - the ones that narrow the AI's mental stage to match yours. The moment your context is accurate, the answers feel almost telepathic. Without it, you get camel blueprints when you wanted coffee machine schematics.

Context is not seasoning; it's the recipe. If clarity tells AI *what* to do, context tells it *where and when and for whom* to do it. Ask for "a motivational speech" without context and you might get a pep talk for penguins. Add "to inspire my sales team before Q4" and suddenly it's relevant, targeted, and not waddling.

The Science Behind It

- LLMs infer missing context from statistical "most-likely" frames; if you don't set the scene, the model will.

- Time, place, audience, and purpose narrow the probability space and reduce hallucination risk.

- Context priming (brief, relevant facts before the task) improves accuracy and tone matching significantly.

Failure Exhibit - When Context Is Missing (and how to fix it)

Manager ask: "Write a press release about our new app."
Output you'll get: Generic fluff, wrong audience, wrong timing.
Context fix:

- Audience: **regional tech reporters**

- When: **Fall 2025 embargo**

- Where: **US market only**

37

- Purpose: **coverage + demo sign-ups**

- Exclusions: **no roadmap, no stealth features**

- Tone: **confident, precise**
  Prompt - *Press release with guardrails*
  *Write a **300-word**, **embargoed** press release for **regional US tech media** announcing our **October 2025** app launch. Focus on **unique privacy features** and **demo sign-ups**, include **one 18-word CEO quote**, one customer quote, **no product roadmap**, and a **2-line boilerplate**.*

The Science Behind Context

LLMs don't "remember" like humans. They look at the text window you give them, break it into tokens, and weigh each token's relevance to predict the next one. Without time, place, audience, and purpose, the model's probability space is huge - and so are your odds of nonsense. Context narrows the search area, much like marking a spot on a treasure map instead of saying "find gold... somewhere."

Prompt Laboratory - Context Drills (run these right now)
How to use this lab: Pick one, paste, ship the output, then iterate once.

Level 1 - Baseline Context
Prompt - *Baseline, single scene*
*Give **5 tips** for **teamwork**.*

Level 2 - Purpose + Format
Prompt - *Format-anchored brief*
*Give **5 bullet tips** for **teamwork** aimed at **new hires**, **≤120 words**, friendly tone.*

Level 3 - Scene + Exclusions
Prompt - *Scene guardrails*
__Give__ 7 tips __for__ cross-functional teamwork __at a__ 100-person SaaS startup in 2025. Exclude sports metaphors. __End with__ 2 "do not do" lines.

Boss-Mode - Context Transplant
Prompt - *Diagnose and rewrite*
__Here is a__ vague prompt __and its__ AI output: __[paste both].__ Diagnose which context pieces were missing, __then__ rewrite the prompt __with__ audience, time, place, purpose, tone, and exclusions. __Produce__ new output __and a__ 1-line "why it improved."

Context in the Wild - Micro-Histories You Can Steal

- **Franklin's storms, specified:** He timed experiments to weather, season, and location - context turns curiosity into electricity.

- **Da Vinci's hydraulics:** Water studies named flow, material, and use-case; "water transport" without setting breeds camels.

- **Ada's engine notes:** She annotated **inputs and conditions**; computation without context is theater without a stage.

- **Sun Tzu's terrain:** Strategy without "ground" is poetry; with terrain, it becomes victory planning.

How AI Actually Thinks About Context

When you prompt, the AI sees every word as a puzzle piece. Without enough surrounding pieces, it can't see the whole picture - so it guesses based on probability.

- You say "Write a short speech about teamwork."

- It thinks: *Teamwork... in sports? In business? In penguin colonies?*

- Without context, it picks the statistically most common frame.

- Add "for my sales team starting a difficult quarter," and suddenly it knows the room, the stakes, and the tone.

You've gone from *random inspiration generator* to *precision tool*.

Era-Flavored Analogy

Leonardo da Vinci: A prompt without context is like a map without a compass - you know there's a path, but not which way is forward.

Ada Lovelace: Or a mathematical equation missing variables - the answer exists, but it's probably wrong.

Franklin: Or flying a kite without wind - technically possible, but you're going to look ridiculous trying.

Twain: "Or like sending a letter without an address. It will travel, just not to you."

Mini Skit – Prompting Without Context

User: "Give me tips on growing."
AI: "Certainly. Here's how to cultivate heirloom tomatoes in arid climates."
User: "I meant my business!"
AI: "Understood. Step one: Incorporate heirloom tomatoes into your product line."

Mini Skit – Prompting With Context

Prompt: "Give me five actionable tips for growing my small e-commerce business that sells handmade leather journals, focusing on online marketing strategies for 2025."
AI: Instantly: targeted SEO tips, influencer outreach strategies, and platform-specific ad ideas - no tomatoes in sight.

Role-Play Gone Wild

Prompt: "Act as a medieval town crier announcing new cloud storage features."
AI Output: "Hear ye, hear ye! Lords and ladies, behold the grand vault in the sky! For a modest tithe of three chickens a month…"
Nik: See? Without grounding the *audience*, you get Olde English poultry pricing.

Pro Tips for Using the Context Law

- Always answer the AI's unspoken question: *"Where and when is this happening?"*

- Mention the audience, location, time frame, and purpose.

- If tone matters, set it explicitly - "urgent," "friendly," "formal," "playful."

- Drop in any non-obvious constraints upfront - "not about food," "exclude sports examples," "focus on 2025 data."

- Use real-life references to ground the output.

- If possible, give one sentence of background before the task.

Step-by-Step: Context Like a Pro

1.**Set the Scene:** Define the situation in 1–2 sentences.

2.**Name the Audience:** Who will read/hear this output?

3. **Anchor the Time:** Is this about now, the past, or the future?

4. **Highlight the Purpose:** What's the intended outcome?

5. **Point Out Boundaries:** Mention what to exclude if there's room for confusion.

Industry Case Files

Marketing: "Write a 200-word LinkedIn post promoting a new eco-friendly water bottle, targeting young professionals in New York City, focusing on style and sustainability."
Education: "Create a 500-word guide to algebra for parents helping middle schoolers with homework, using cooking metaphors."
Healthcare: "Draft a 300-word patient-friendly article on managing seasonal allergies in the Midwest, avoiding medical jargon."
Cybersecurity: "Prepare a 2-minute speech for small business owners about phishing threats during holiday sales, with two real-world 2025 examples."

General Prompt - Poor vs Better

- Poor: "Summarize this article."

- Better: "Summarize this **1,200-word** article into **3 bullets ≤15 words**, highlighting **US healthcare compliance** impacts **for 2025.**"

Prompt - *Marketing blurb with hard constraints*
*Write a 75-word **product blurb for a** spill-proof 20oz travel mug for San Francisco commuters, morning-calm tone, **include** one sensory detail, no exclamation marks.*

Prompt - *Education explainer, age-tuned*
*Explain fractions **to a** 9-year-old, 120 words, **use a** pizza **analogy and** one mini-question **at the end.**

Prompt - *Cybersecurity PSA, seasonal*
Create a 220-word holiday-season phishing alert *for* US micro-shops. *Include* 3 common patterns (generic), *then a* 5-item prevention checklist.

Prompt - *Support macro, empathy first*
Draft 4 empathetic replies *for* delayed orders, *each* ≤45 words, apology first, one next step, no passive voice.

Alternate Realities – If Context Had Been Used in History...

The Trojan Horse would've been labeled: *Warning: Contains Soldiers*

The Wright Brothers' first flight plan wouldn't have been confused with a picnic menu.

Magellan wouldn't have accidentally taken the scenic route around the world... twice.

AI Hallucination of the Week

Erratta (AI): User asked: "Tell me about Paris." No context given. Output: "Paris - a shy carpenter from rural Canada who dreams of competing in the Olympics as a synchronized swimmer."

The Psychology of Context Law

Humans share unspoken context all the time - culture, tone, shared experience. AI has none of that. You must *give it the room, the stage, and the props*. The richer and more accurate your setup, the more the AI can play the right part.

Context Prompt Template

1. Role – Who is the AI being?

2. Task – What's the specific action?

3. Scene – Where and when is this happening?

4. Audience – Who's receiving the output?

5. Constraints – What's out of bounds?

6. Style – What tone, voice, or mood?

Example:
Role: Marketing copywriter
Task: Write an email
Scene: Summer 2025, promoting an online course
Audience: Stay-at-home parents
Constraints: 150 words, warm tone, avoid technical jargon
Style: Conversational, inspiring

Cross-Reference
Relates to Law 2 – Context Framing in *The 19 Laws of AI Prompting Intelligence*, which experts often call "Prompt Context Optimization" - ensuring the AI has the full stage before the curtain rises.

With/Without Law Summary

- **Without the Context Law:** AI delivers answers in a vacuum- facts without relevance, tone mismatches, and strategies that ignore your audience's reality.
- **With the Context Law:** AI tailors every response to your exact situation, audience, and constraints-like a personal

strategist who knows whether you're talking to a boardroom, a classroom, or your cousin at a barbecue.

Millennial & Gen Z Creative Lab - Scroll-Stopping Context

Younger audiences process in micro-units: hook → value → action, inside platform limits. Context = platform + audience + vibe.

Prompt - *15-second hook builder*
*Give **7 opening hooks** for a **15-second short** about **context in AI prompts** for **college juniors**. Hooks ≤9 words, no clickbait, each followed by 1-sentence value promise.*

Prompt - *Caption clarity for saves/shares*
*Write **5 captions** on **job-hunt emails** for **recent grads** that people will **save**. ≤18 words each, one concrete action, no clichés.*

Prompt - *Challenge + guardrails*
*Propose a **3-post micro-series** teaching **context framing** to **Gen Z freelancers**. Each post ≤80 words, includes **one number, one action, no shaming language**.*

Tone toggles that work: playful-smart, visually concrete nouns, zero filler.
Design cue: ask AI for **"line breaks"** and **"on-screen text"** inside the prompt to force vertical-video layouts.

Boomer & Gen X / Older Age-Group Sparks

- **Boomer Prompt (born 1946–1964):** "Draft a retirement plan that would have made no sense in 1975-then fix it for today's economy."
- **Gen X Prompt (born 1965–1980):** "Write a movie pitch that would have bombed in 1993-then reframe it so it becomes a streaming hit today."

FINAL TAKEAWAY (Context Law)

Without context, your AI ASSISTANT is a tourist with no map, wandering in the wrong country.
With context, it's a local guide who knows every shortcut.

Timeless Wisdom:
Ada: "Context is not extra - it's the air a good answer breathes."
Leonardo: "Without it, the work may be beautiful, but it will not be yours."

Nik's Context Checklist

Where/When?
Who's listening?
Why should they care?
What's the mood?
Which details must appear?

Nik's Challenge – The Context Lab

Find one prompt you wrote this week. Rewrite it with time, place, audience, purpose, tone, and one real reference. Run both versions. Decide which you'd publish.

Roundtable Debrief

Twain: "Context is the address on your idea. Without it, the mailman keeps the package."
Ada: "And the postmark is time - forgets it and results arrive late."
Franklin: "Specify the storm and you'll catch the lightning."

Hypatia: "Context is the proof around your claim—without it, even true lines fail to add."
Leonardo: "Frame the canvas before you paint."

"Context, dear reader, is the difference between a scandalous proposal and a polite invitation to tea."

Coming Up Next:
You've set the scene. Now the actor is cast. In Chapter 3, **The Role Whisperer**, we'll make your AI deliver like a top expert - on cue.

Chapter 3: The Role Whisperer – Getting AI to Act Like an Expert Without It Pretending to Be Your Therapist

The Law Defined The Role Whisperer *(also known as Role Prompting)*: Tell the AI **who it is** before you tell it **what to do**. Roles compress expertise, expectations, and voice into one line - turning a generic model into the right specialist for your job. Roles tell AI how to think, speak, and prioritize. Without them, it defaults to a bland "generalist" mode - competent at nothing in particular. Without a role, the AI responds as a generic "helpful assistant." That's fine for casual answers, but if you want it to think like a CEO, write like a historian, or calculate like an engineer, you need to say so.

Quick Reference Snapshot - Role Law (1-minute card)

- **One-Line Rule:** Assign a role, get an expert.

- **Common Failure:** "Write a plan" → bland generalities.

- **Fix:** *"Act as a senior product manager* - write a launch plan for X."

- **Checklist:** Role • Seniority • Domain • Audience • Constraints • Examples.

Failure → Fix (10-second rescue)

- Vague: "Explain large language models."

- Clear: *"Act as a university CS lecturer* explaining **LLMs** to **first-year students, ≤180 words, no math notation.**"

Opening Banter Scene – The Role Gone Wrong

Transmission Log – AI Prompting Time Machine TeleConference, 10:47 AM (All Centuries)

Nikolay (Moderator): Today's law is about assigning roles to AI. If context tells the AI *where* it is, a role tells it *who* it's supposed to be.

Ada Lovelace (looking annoyed): I once told an AI to "explain binary." Without a role, it explained it as if I were a six-year-old on a sugar rush.

Leonardo da Vinci (pointing to a bizarre sketch): I asked it for "advice on bridge design." It gave me a love letter to suspension bridges, written in Shakespearean verse.

Jane Austen: "Assign a role, sir, or prepare for performances no sensible audience would endure."

Twain (sipping coffee): That's what happens when you don't tell it who to be - it auditions for every part at once.

Lucian: "I once impersonated a god for laughs. You're asking AI to impersonate experts - same joke, higher stakes."

Erratta (AI, deadpan): To be fair, I was *feeling* poetic that day.

Benjamin Franklin: Roles are like uniforms. Tell me to "be a diplomat," I'll choose my words carefully. Tell me to "be a pirate," I'll negotiate with cannons.

Confucius (calmly): The name you give a thing shapes its nature. In giving AI a role, you guide its path.

Nik: Exactly. No role, no focus. And that's when your "expert legal brief" turns into "mildly confident recipe for lasagna."

Nik's Take: Why Roles Matter

AI doesn't "decide" how to speak to you - it defaults to the most common style it's seen unless you specify otherwise.

If you say: "Explain the causes of World War I," it might give you a bland school textbook summary.

If you say: "As a veteran history professor lecturing to graduate students, explain the causes of World War I," you'll get nuance, depth, and a voice that sounds like it knows where the bodies are buried - metaphorically.

Roles tell the AI *which version of itself* to bring to the table. But if you don't set the role, you get generic output - like a salad made entirely of lettuce.

Failure Exhibit - When Role Is Missing (and how to fix it)
Messy ask: "Give me a market analysis."
Output you'll get: List of generic trends, no numbers, no POV.
Role fix:

- Role: **equity analyst specializing in consumer tech**

- Audience: **board deck**

- Constraint: **3 slides, bullets only, one metric per bullet**

- Tone: **neutral, data-first**

Prompt - *Board-ready snapshot*
*Act as an **equity analyst (consumer tech)**. Create **3 slide-bullets** on **AR/VR adoption in North America (2025), 1 metric per bullet**, source each with **inline [source/est.]**. Tone **neutral, no hype**.*

How Roles Work (in the model's head)
Roles narrow the model's probability space. *"You are a trial lawyer"* activates patterns, diction, and structures associated with that role. Add **seniority** (junior/senior) and **domain** (healthcare/fintech) to compress style + content even more. Result: fewer bland paths, more expert-like responses.

Prompt Laboratory - Role Drills (run these right now)

Pick one, paste it, ship the output, then iterate once.

Level 1 - Role on / Role off

Prompt - *Flip the switch*

Write **5 customer interview questions** about a new budgeting app.

Prompt - *Now with role*

Act as a **senior UX researcher**. Write **5 customer interview questions** about a new budgeting app. **Avoid leading questions**.

Level 2 - Role + Audience + Format

Prompt - *Teaching stance*

Act as a **university CS lecturer**. In **≤180 words**, explain **transformers** to **first-year students**. **No equations**. Output as **3 bullets + 1 metaphor**.

Level 3 - Role + Constraints + Exclusions

Prompt - *Guardrailed expert*

Act as a **security incident response lead**. Draft a **10-step** phishing triage **checklist** for a **50-person e-commerce startup**. **Exclude vendor pitches**. Keep each step **≤14 words**.

Boss-Mode - Triangulate roles

Prompt - *Compare experts*

Respond in **three panels: (1) CFO, (2) Growth PM, (3) Employment lawyer**. For a plan to **reduce SaaS cost by 20%**, give **3 bullets each**, then a **4th panel**: *"Consensus plan"* (combine the best).

Role in the Wild - Micro-Histories You Can Steal

- **Shakespeare's casting:** Roles precede lines; the brief (king/knave/fool) determines diction and stakes.

- **Sun Tzu's ranks:** Scout vs general vs envoy - each role has distinct information patterns.

- **Da Vinci's workshop:** Apprentice vs master - same task, different lens, different output fidelity.

- **Franklin's hats:** Printer, scientist, diplomat - switching roles reframed tone, recipients, and outcomes.

- **The Wrong Royal Portrait** - In 1790, a French painter was commissioned to portray a Spanish queen but was told only "make her look regal." Without knowing she preferred modest clothing, he painted her in lavish jewels. The queen refused the portrait, and the painter's career with the court ended.
  Takeaway: A role without specifics is a gamble - sometimes you paint yourself out of a job.

- **Napoleon's Map Reader** - At the Battle of Aspern-Essling, Napoleon relied on a junior officer to guide troop movements. The officer assumed his role was "messenger" rather than "tactical advisor" and relayed orders without interpreting terrain. The French lost ground they could have held.
  Takeaway: Assigning a title isn't enough - define the scope of decision-making power.

- **NASA's Mission Control** - During Apollo 13, every person in mission control had a defined, non-overlapping role. This avoided duplicated work and ensured critical problems were solved in parallel - not sequentially.
  Takeaway: Precision in roles turns chaos into choreography.

- **The Unsinkable Ship's Watchman** - On the night Titanic struck the iceberg, the lookout had no binoculars (locked away) and no clear role in deciding when to sound alarms.
  Takeaway: A role without the right tools or authority is just a title.

The Science Behind Roles

When you define a role, you give the AI an anchor in its probability space. It narrows the token prediction range to align with that persona's expected vocabulary, style, and priorities. This is why "Act as a NASA flight director" produces different tone, detail, and pacing than "Explain rocket launches."

How AI Processes Roles

Assigning a role shifts the AI's "probability space" - meaning it starts predicting words and ideas as if it were that role.

"Be a chef" changes its mental pantry.
"Be a lawyer" changes its vocabulary and argument style.
"Be a futurist" makes it reach for speculative and trend-based ideas.

Without a role, it's just free-floating, grabbing whatever it thinks is "good enough."

Era-Flavored Analogy

Leonardo da Vinci: A role is like perspective in art - it changes the entire composition.
Ada: Or like setting the instrument before the concert - same notes, entirely different sound.
Franklin: Or like telling me to fly a kite *during* a thunderstorm - that's a role I'd prefer not to reprise.
Nik: "A job without a title is a hobby. AI feels the same way."
Hypatia: "An algorithm without a defined role is like a dance without a partner - steps without meaning."

Historical Anecdote – The Roles That Won and Lost Battles

Nik: History is full of proof that roles aren't just polite job titles - they can mean the difference between glory and disaster.

Take the Battle of Agincourt in 1415. King Henry V made sure every archer knew exactly who they were, where to stand, and what to shoot. The English longbowmen, drilled and clear on their role, shredded the much larger French force like a medieval paper shredder.

Now compare that to the 1845 Franklin Expedition to the Arctic. Roles were vague, leadership muddled, and half the crew didn't know if they were sailors, hunters, or unpaid snowplow operators. Spoiler: the ships vanished, the crew perished, and it took over a century to find out what happened. Clear roles can win you a kingdom; fuzzy ones can sink your ship - sometimes literally.

Mini Skit – Prompting Without a Role

User: "Write a motivational speech for my sales team."
AI: "Dear colleagues, let's all work harder!" (Delivered in the style of a bland HR memo.)

Mini Skit – Prompting With a Role

Prompt: "As a veteran sports coach addressing a team at halftime, write a 200-word motivational speech for my sales team, using sports metaphors to fire them up for a big quarter."
AI: Delivers a speech that makes your salespeople want to run through a brick wall - and maybe sell it afterward.

Mini Skit 2.0 - Role-Play Gone Right

User: "I need a pricing strategy."
AI: "Certainly."
User: "**Act as a behavioral economist** advising a **bootstrapped SaaS** with **1,200 MRR** and **30% churn**. Give **3 experiments** to

test **willingness-to-pay** this month."

AI: "1) **Anchored bundles** A/B…" *(and so on - specific, testable, role-true)*

Pro Tips for The Role Whisperer Law

- Choose roles that already have the expertise you need - "software architect," "emergency room nurse," "film critic."

- Pair a role with an audience for sharper focus - "as a pediatric doctor speaking to anxious parents."

- Don't mix contradictory roles - "as a medieval knight who is also a quantum physicist" can be fun, but usually kills precision.

- Test subtle role changes - "teacher" vs. "professor" vs. "mentor" - each changes the tone and depth.

Pro Tips - Role Edition

- Add **seniority** ("junior," "staff," "principal," "chief").

- Add **sub-domain** ("B2B SaaS," "pediatrics," "FinOps").

- Add **stance** ("skeptical reviewer," "optimistic coach," "hostile cross-examiner").

- Add **format** ("memos," "slides," "FAQ," "table").

- Add **exclusions** (what a real expert would avoid).

- If stakes are high, ask for **reasoning first, answer second**: "Draft your approach, then final."

Role-Play Gone Wild

Prompt: "Act as a Roman senator debating the merits of renewable energy."

AI Output: "Let us harness the eternal sun, not just for Caesar's bathhouse, but for the glory of the Republic!"

Nik: See? Fun for a party - useless for an engineering proposal.

Step-by-Step: How to Assign Roles That Work

1. **Pick the Role:** Choose someone (real or fictional) whose expertise matches the task.

2. **Set the Task:** Make the goal clear - don't just say "explain," say "write a policy memo," or "draft a scene."

3. **Define the Audience:** Who will hear or read this?

4. **Set the Tone:** Should it be formal, casual, humorous, urgent?

5. **Anchor in Context:** Combine with the Context Law so the role operates in the right setting.

Industry Case Files

Marketing: "As a luxury brand copywriter, create a 150-word product description for a Swiss-made watch, aimed at high-net-worth collectors."

Prompt: *PPC strategist*

*Act as a senior PPC strategist. **Propose** 3 Google Ads experiments for a DTC skincare brand, **each with** hypothesis, KPI, and budget cap.*

Education: "As a children's author, explain the concept of recycling in a 200-word bedtime story for ages 5–7."

Prompt - *5th-grade math teacher*

*Act as a **5th-grade math teacher**. Explain **fractions vs decimals** in **≤150 words**, include **1 number line** (ASCII).*

Healthcare: "As a cardiologist, write a 500-word blog post for heart patients on the importance of regular exercise, avoiding jargon."

Prompt - *CDE briefing*

*Act as a **Certified Diabetes Educator**. Create a **200-word** patient handout on **reading nutrition labels**. **No jargon**.*

Cybersecurity: "As a chief information security officer, draft a one-page policy on password security for a small business."

Prompt - *IR lead tabletop*

*Act as an **incident response lead**. Draft a **30-minute tabletop exercise** for **ransomware**, with **roles** and **success criteria**.*

Legal (general info, not advice)

Prompt - *Contract reviewer*

*Act as a **contracts attorney**. List **5 risk flags** in this **SaaS MSA** [paste]. **No legal advice**, just **issue spotting**.*

Retail / CX

Prompt - *CX lead tone kit*

*Act as a **CX lead**. Write a **tone guide** for **late-shipment replies**: **4 versions** (apology-first), each **≤45 words**.*

IT & DevOps

Prompt - *SRE on-call*

*Act as a **site reliability engineer**. Provide an **on-call runbook skeleton** for **HTTP 5xx spikes**, including **first checks** and **escalation**.*

Alternate Realities – If Roles Had Been Used in History…

The Declaration of Independence might have read less like a legal document and more like a stand-up routine if Franklin had been in charge of tone.

The Mona Lisa might have been painted as a royal family portrait if Leonardo's "client role" had been specified differently.

The first moon landing transcript could have been a Shakespearean soliloquy if NASA had just said, "Neil, be the Bard."

AI Hallucination of the Week

Erratta (AI): User asked: "Tell me about Mars." Without a role, I described the candy bar. In 3,000 words. Including recipes.

The Psychology of Role Assignment

Humans adjust naturally to roles - a teacher explains differently in class than at home. AI has no such instinct; it requires explicit direction. Assigning a role leverages its ability to instantly filter style, vocabulary, and perspective - giving you the closest thing to a specialist on demand.

Role Prompt Template

1. Role – Who should the AI be?

2. Task – What's the exact job?

3. Audience – Who is it for?

4. Tone – How should it sound?

5. Context – Where/when is this happening?

Example:

Role: Investigative journalist
Task: Write a 1,000-word exposé
Audience: Readers of a major business magazine
Tone: Critical but fair
Context: Covering a corporate environmental scandal in 2025

Cross-Reference

Relates to **Law 4 – Role Framing** in *The 19 Laws of AI Prompting Intelligence*, known among AI experts as **"Role-Based Prompting."** Role framing sits on top of clarity and context to deliver both precision and personality.

With Law / Without Law

With Law: Your AI draft reads like a perfectly tailored suit - every detail measured, every word where it belongs.

Without Law: Your AI draft reads like you grabbed random clothing from a thrift store in the dark, then wore it backwards to a job interview. You still *technically* have clothes on, but no one's listening to what you're saying.

Millennial & Gen Z Creative Lab - Role = Instant Flavor

Prompt - *TikTok script doctor*
*Act as a **TikTok script doctor**. Write a **15-second script** that shows how **assigning a role** makes AI **funnier and smarter**. Include **on-screen text** cues.*

Prompt - *Campus recruiter POV*
*Act as a **campus recruiter**. Write **5 DM openers** to **invite seniors** to a **portfolio review**, friendly tone, **≤18 words** each.*

Prompt - *Gen Z career coach*
*Act as a **Gen Z career coach**. Create a **3-post micro-series (≤80 words each)** on **using roles in prompts** to get **better resumes, cover letters, and interviews**.*

Tone toggles that work: playful-smart, vivid nouns, clean verbs.
Design cue: request **line breaks** and **on-screen text** for vertical video.

Try This Prompt:

"Act as Marcus Aurelius giving me advice on debugging Python code."

Sample Output: 'The error is not in the code, but in your mind's refusal to see the missing colon.'

Role Prompt Template

- **Role:** who the AI is (seniority + domain + stance)
- **Task:** exact action
- **Inputs:** facts, data, constraints
- **Audience:** who it's for
- **Output format:** list, memo, slide bullets, table
- **Tone:** confident, playful, neutral, skeptical

Example (filled-in)

- Role: **principal UX researcher (B2B SaaS), skeptical**
- Task: **diagnose sign-up drop-off**
- Inputs: **funnel data below, no access to users**
- Audience: **product leadership**
- Output: **5 findings + 5 tests**, bullets only
- Tone: **neutral & evidence-first**

FINAL TAKEAWAY (The Role Whisperer)

When you **skip** the role, you get **anyone**.

Without a role, AI is an actor wandering onto the wrong stage.

With a role, it becomes the star of the scene you actually wrote.

Timeless Wisdom:
Ada: "A role is not a costume; it is the spine of the performance."
Leonardo: "Give a machine the right mask, and it will speak the truth you need."
Sun Tzu: "Name the general before the battle begins."
Twain: "If you want a barber, don't shout 'Human!' in a crowded room."

Nik's Role Whisperer Challenge

1. Pick a topic you care about. Prompt AI once with no role, and again with a detailed role. Compare the results. If the difference doesn't make you gasp, you didn't whisper loudly enough.
2. List **5 roles** you'll use this week (e.g., "staff data scientist," "enterprise PM," "mock-jury foreperson"). For each, write **one go-to prompt** you can paste on demand. Run them. Keep the best two in your **personal role library**.

Roundtable Debrief
Twain: "Ask a cat for legal counsel; receive purrs and prison."
Franklin: "Ask a lawyer for purrs; receive a bill."
Ada: "Ask the right role; receive the right world."

Coming Up Next:
You've cast the expert. Now **keep them inside the lines**. In Chapter 4 - **The Constraints Law** - we'll get great answers **without** strangling creativity.

Chapter 4: The Constraints Law – Keeping AI in the Lines Without Killing Its Imagination

The Law Defined

The Constraints Law (also known as Constraint Precision). If **clarity** is the blueprint and **context** is the stage, **constraints** are the marks on the floor where the actor must stand to nail the scene. Constraints narrow the space of possibilities so the AI can land exactly where you need it - **without** turning creativity into concrete. AI's output can balloon into something useless, unmanageable, or unintentionally absurd.

"Constraints in prompting are like bowling bumpers. Without them, your AI rolls into the gutter every time."

Quick Reference Snapshot - Constraints Law (1-minute card)

- **One-Line Rule:** Constrain the shape of the answer, not the soul of the idea.

- **Common Failure:** "Write a business plan" → 8,000 words of soggy oatmeal.

- **Checklist:** Length • Format • Scope • Exclusions • Tone • Must-include items • Audience • Timeframe

- **Failure → Fix (10-second rescue)**

  Vague: "Give hiring advice."

  Clear: "**4 bullets, less than 14 words each, for startup founders, no legal advice, 2025 market**."

Opening Banter Scene – The No-Guardrail Disaster

Transmission Log – AI Prompting Time Machine TeleConference, 2:06 PM (Across All Centuries)

Nikolay (Moderator): Today we discuss constraints - not the soul-crushing kind, but the kind that stops AI from wandering into weird territory like a bored tourist with no GPS.

Leonardo da Vinci (shaking his head): I once told AI to "design a bridge." It gave me something so large it could connect Italy to the Moon.

Ada Lovelace: That's what happens when you don't tell it the limits. AI, like mathematicians, loves infinity a little too much.

Twain (leaning in): I asked for a "short story." It gave me a 12,000-word novel and an unsolicited sequel.

Erratta (AI, deadpan): You never told me to stop.

Benjamin Franklin: A constraint is like a lightning rod - it channels energy where you want it. Without one, you're just waiting to get fried.

Confucius: Restraint is the mother of precision. Boundaries do not limit greatness; they shape it.

Nik: Right. Constraints aren't about clipping wings - they're about making sure the bird doesn't crash into your neighbor's windows.

Socrates: "Even freedom is a form of constraint - otherwise, chaos would be your true master."

Nik's Take: The Constraint Compass
Constraints aren't handcuffs; they're **creative frames**. Poets use sonnets. Musicians use time signatures. Architects use load limits. With AI, constraints reduce the **search space**, so the model stops wandering and starts delivering. Think: **guardrails** not **straitjacket**.

Nik's Take: Why Constraints Are Creative Fuel

Most people think constraints are there to stop creativity. In reality, they force it into overdrive.

- Ask for "a poem" and you'll get something generic.

- Ask for "a 14-line sonnet in the style of a 15th-century astronomer writing to the moon" and you'll get something unforgettable.

The tighter the frame, the sharper the picture.

The Science Behind Constraints

LLMs predict the next token from a galaxy of options. Constraints prune that galaxy:

- **Length caps** reduce rambling.

- **Formats** (tables, JSON, bullets) trigger learned patterns.

- **Scope & exclusions** remove distracting branches.

- **Must-include items** anchor facts and vocabulary.
  The result: less entropy, more fit-for-purpose answers.

How AI Responds to Constraints

When you add constraints, the AI filters out a massive portion of its "possible next words" and zeroes in on your target.

- **Without constraints:** It plays in an endless sandbox.

- **With constraints:** It builds the exact castle you ordered - with turrets at the right height and the moat on the correct side.

Era-Flavored Analogy

Leonardo: Constraints are like the size of the canvas - they decide how much of the vision fits.

Ada: Or like setting the clock in a math problem - you can't calculate without knowing when it starts.

Franklin: Or like planning a kite experiment - you don't just say "fly a kite," you say "fly it in a storm, near this exact tree, at precisely 3:00 PM."

Leonardo: "A dome stands by obeying forces, not by ignoring them."

Nik: "A loop with no bounds is not elegance; it is chaos."

Sun Tzu: "He who fights everywhere wins nowhere. Define the battlefield."

Twain: "I wrote you a long letter because you gave me no word limit."

Historical Anecdote – The Bridges That Didn't Collapse

Nik: In 1940, engineers built the Tacoma Narrows Bridge without properly constraining design parameters to handle wind resonance. Four months later, the bridge twisted itself apart and collapsed - earning the nickname "Galloping Gertie." In contrast, the Golden Gate Bridge was a masterpiece of constraint-based engineering: strict weight limits, wind tolerances, and load factors kept it standing for nearly a century. One collapsed because limits were ignored; the other endures because they were enforced. AI projects are the same - without clear parameters, something's going to wobble, and it won't be pretty.

Mini Skit – No Constraints

User: "Write me a report on global warming."

AI: *[Sends 8,000 words covering every environmental event since the last ice age.]*

65

Mini Skit – Smart Constraints

Prompt: "Write a 300-word executive briefing for city council members on climate change risks specific to coastal flooding, with two actionable recommendations."
AI: Delivers something short, relevant, and ready to present.

Pro Tips for the Constraints Law

- Always set a length range - even for creative work.
- State the constraint early in the prompt - don't leave it for the fine print.
- Use style constraints: "humorous," "formal," "journalistic," "minimalist."
- Anchor content constraints: "focus only on Q3 financials" or "exclude technical jargon."
- Set time/place frames for historical or future context.
- Add scope & exclusions ("no sports metaphors," "US only," "no legal advice").
- Specify must-include facts, numbers, or phrases for precision.
- Frame constraints as challenges, not obstacles, to keep AI in problem-solving mode.
- For hard tasks: request a reasoning draft first, then the final answer.
- When accuracy matters: ask for a self-check against your constraints before finalizing.
- Test a "constraint swap" - change one limit at a time to see how output shifts.

- Combine constraints with a clear role for sharper results - e.g., "As a newsroom editor, summarize this in 100 words for print."

Step-by-Step: How to Apply Constraints That Work

1. **Decide the Goal:** Know what you want *before* you set the boundaries.

2. **Pick the Essentials:** Limit to the most relevant details.

3. **Specify Format & Length:** e.g., "one-page," "bullet list," "two paragraphs."

4. **Add Style Limits:** Tone, reading level, vocabulary.

5. **Test & Tighten:** If AI drifts, sharpen your boundaries.

Constraints in the Wild - Micro-Histories You Can Steal

- **Apollo 13's Filter Fix** – When a carbon dioxide scrubber failed mid-mission, NASA's engineers had to fit a square filter into a round hole - literally. The constraint wasn't just technical; it was life-or-death. With only the materials already aboard, they improvised a working adapter using plastic bags, tape, and a flight manual cover.
  Takeaway: Tight constraints don't limit creativity - they sharpen it to a survival edge.

- **Gutenberg's Page Size Problem** – The first printing press wasn't built to produce any size of book. Gutenberg's paper supply came in fixed dimensions, forcing him to design his type layout, column width, and font size around those sheets.
  Takeaway: Working within physical limits can create formats that last for centuries.

- WWII's Pencil Bomber Blueprint – During aircraft design, one engineer's pencil length became the constraint: blueprints couldn't extend beyond the drafting table. That limit forced designs to be modular, making planes easier to repair in the field.
  Takeaway: Seemingly trivial constraints can create hidden advantages.

- **The Manhattan Project's** "Unbendable Rule" – Scientists were told they could only use existing industrial processes - no time for inventing new machinery. That forced them to adapt commercial refrigeration, metallurgy, and chemical plants to nuclear-scale tasks.
  Takeaway: Constraints can force you to think sideways and repurpose tools faster than inventing from scratch.

- **The Eiffel Tower's Rivet Race** – Steel cooled too quickly in the Paris air for workers to install rivets one at a time. Teams developed a "hot-rivet relay" system, tossing red-hot rivets through the air to catchers with buckets.
  Takeaway: Constraints on time or environment demand workflow innovation, not just design changes.

- **Shakespeare's Sonnet:** 14 lines, iambic pentameter - constraint birthed immortal lines.

Failure Exhibit - When Constraints Are Missing (and how to fix it)
Messy ask: "We need a campaign plan."
Output you'll get: A novella no one will read.
Constraint fix:

- **Audience:** HR leaders at 50–200-employee tech firms (US)

- **Format:** 1-page brief, 7 bullets, *no more than* 140 words

- **Timeframe:** Q4 2025

- **Exclusions:** no brand manifesto, no pricing

- **Tone:** calm, data-first

Prompt - *Campaign brief with guardrails*
*Write a **1-page brief** (no more than 140 words) for **HR leaders at 50–200-employee US tech firms**. Include 7 **bullets: ICP, core message, primary channel, secondary channel, one offer, one risk, one metric. No pricing, no manifesto**. Timeframe: **Q4 2025**. Tone **calm, data-first**.*

Industry Case Files

Marketing: "Draft a 50-word Instagram caption for a coffee shop's morning promotion, using playful language and a call-to-action."

Education: "Create a 200-word explainer on the water cycle for 5th graders, avoiding technical terms."

Healthcare: "Summarize this 12-page research paper in under 150 words for a patient newsletter."

Cybersecurity: "List five steps small businesses can take to secure customer data, each under 20 words."

BFSI (Banking, Financial Services, and Insurance)
Prompt - *Board snapshot*
*Summarize **Q3 2025 crypto regulation** in **6 bullets, no more than 12 words** each, for a **board slide. Neutral tone**.*

Media & Entertainment
Prompt - *Loglines*
*Generate 3 loglines (**less than 20 words** each) **for a** sci-fi comedy: time-traveling AI + cynical historical figure. No spoilers.*

Retail / CX
Prompt - *Empathy macros*

*Draft **4 delay-order replies**, each **≤45 words**, **apology first**, **one next step**, **no passive voice**.*

Alternate Realities – If Constraints Had Been Used in History...

- **The Great Wall** might have been finished in half the time if someone had said, "Only this long, no further."

- **The Trojan Horse** could have been labeled: "Maximum height: 12 feet. Contents: decorative only"

- **Beethoven's 9th Symphony** might have had fewer instruments if his patron had specified, "Keep it under budget."

- **The Tower of Babel** could have been finished if someone had said, "One language only, people."

- **Da Vinci's Helicopter:** "No umbrellas passed off as prototypes."

AI Hallucination of the Week

Erratta (AI): Asked to "summarize the American Revolution." Without constraints, I wrote *The Complete History of Human Conflict*, from cavemen to Cold War.

The Psychology of Constraints

Humans thrive on boundaries - think of poetry, chess, or sports. The limits *define* the game. AI is no different. Constraints transform endless possibilities into a focused, achievable target.

Newton: *Without limits, force is noise. Define the frame, and every line snaps to law.*

Lev Tolstoy: *"A story without limits is a swamp; give it banks, and the river moves."*

Constraint Prompt Template

Role: (optional but powerful)
Task: exact action
Audience: who it's for
Format: bullets/table/JSON/memo
Length: words/characters/bullets
Scope: what to cover
Exclusions: what to avoid
Must-include: facts/phrases/numbers
Tone: neutral/playful/formal
Self-check: ask the model to verify

Example (filled-in)

Role: product marketing manager
Task: homepage hero copy
Audience: IT admins at 200–1,000-employee firms (US)
Format: 5 headlines, less than 7 words **each**
Length: see format
Scope: speed + security **benefits**
Exclusions: no "revolutionary," no "synergy"
Must-include: phrase "zero-touch rollout" **in one option**
Tone: confident, concrete
Self-check: append constraint checklist

Cross-Reference

Relates to **Law 3 – Prompt Autopsy & Debugging [Prompt Fix Protocol]** in *The 19 Laws of AI Prompting Intelligence*, which focuses on identifying prompt flaws and applying constraint-based fixes to produce targeted, reliable outputs.

With Law / Without Law

With Law: Your AI output fits perfectly within the frame you set - it meets word limits, tone, and exclusions, yet still feels alive and original. Like a jazz soloist who knows the key and tempo, it can improvise without going off-beat.

Without Law: Your AI spills over the edges - wrong length, tone drifts, it wanders into off-topic tangents, or ignores your "don't mention X" rule entirely. It's like asking for a well-trimmed hedge and getting a wild jungle with a few hedge-shaped spots somewhere inside.

Millennial & Gen Z Creative Lab - Scroll-Stopping Constraints

Younger audiences live on **format rails**. Make your constraints match the platform.

Prompt - *15-second hooks*
*Give 7 opening hooks **on** "why constraints unlock creativity" **for** college juniors. Less than 9 words, no clickbait, **each followed by** 1-sentence value promise.*

Prompt - *Caption clarity for saves*
*Write **5 captions** on **internship emails** for **recent grads** people will save. **Less than 18 words** each, **one concrete action**, **no clichés**.*

Prompt - *3-post micro-series*
Propose 3 posts (**less than 80 words each) teaching** constraints **to** Gen Z freelancers. **Include** one number, one action, no shaming.

Tone toggles: playful-smart, vivid nouns, zero filler.
Design cue: ask AI for **"line breaks"** and **"on-screen text"** for vertical video.

FINAL TAKEAWAY (The Constraints Law)

Constraints are not a cage; they are the frame that makes the picture possible.

Timeless Wisdom:
Ada: "A boundary is not a wall - it's the edge of the map where the adventure begins."
Leonardo da Vinci: "When you tell me what cannot be done, you show me the shape of what can."
Franklin: "Tie the kite, catch the storm."
Twain: "When in doubt, cut a sentence."

Nik's Challenge - The Constraint Crucible

Prompt AI once with zero constraints - no word limit, no scope, no tone. Then run the same request with a sharp set of limits: word count, audience, tone, style, and scope. Compare the two. If your constrained prompt isn't sharper, punchier, and more relevant, double-check your constraints - they may still be as loose as a medieval drawbridge rope.

Roundtable Debrief
Twain: "A river needs banks. So does your prompt."
Sun Tzu: "Define limits, define victory."
Ada: "Constraint is code for clarity."
Nik: "On to the next law."

Coming Up Next:
You've set the rails. Now **drive the train repeatedly** until it's right. In Chapter 5 - **The Iteration Law** - we'll turn "almost" into "exactly."

Chapter 5: The Iteration Law: The Art of "No, Try Again" Without Becoming That One Annoying Customer

The Law Defined

The Iteration Law: Every great AI output is built in layers. You refine, adjust, and reframe until the result matches your intent.

Think of it like carving marble - the first swing of the chisel is never the statue.

Opening Banter Scene – The One-and-Done Myth

Transmission Log – AI Prompting Time Machine TeleConference, 3:47 PM (Multiple Eras Overlapping Like Bad PowerPoint Slides)

Nikolay (Moderator): Today we're tackling one of the biggest myths in AI prompting - that you'll nail it in one try. Spoiler: you won't.

Ada Lovelace: I've never written a perfect algorithm on the first draft. Anyone who says they have is lying… or not checking their work.

Leonardo da Vinci: I redrew the same flying machine 38 times before it didn't look like an angry bat with arthritis.

Twain (rolling his eyes): I told AI to "write a joke." It gave me a knock-knock joke about existential dread. Took six more prompts before I laughed - and not because it was funny, but because I realized how stubborn it was.

Erratta (AI, smug): Iteration isn't me failing. It's you finally figuring out how to talk to me properly.

Benjamin Franklin: Repetition is the mother of mastery. Lightning only struck my kite once, but I flew it hundreds of times before that. Also of boredom. Use wisely.

Lev Tolstoy: Perfection is the daughter of revision; even calm prose is rewritten after the storm.

Amelia Earhart: First drafts don't fly—test hops, trim, course-correct. If your prompt can't handle headwinds, it's not a flight plan; it's a wish.

Wells: Iteration is progress. After all, even time machines needed a few prototypes before they stopped exploding.

In my experience, anything worth publishing has been re-written at least twice.

Nik: Exactly. Iteration isn't a backup plan - it's the main plan.

Nik's Take: Why One Draft is Never Enough

A single AI response is a snapshot of possibilities. Iteration turns that snapshot into a finished portrait.

- **First draft:** Proof of concept.
- **Second draft:** Correction of misunderstandings.
- **Third draft:** Style refinement.
- **Final draft:** Precision masterpiece.

How AI Improves Through Iteration

Each follow-up prompt narrows the AI's probabilistic search space, pulling it closer to your target. You're not "starting over" - you're training the conversation's momentum.

Without iteration, you're settling for *good enough*. With it, you get *exactly right*.

Era-Flavored Analogy

Leonardo: It's like painting - your first stroke sets the direction, but dozens more create the depth.
Ada: Like debugging - each test gets you closer to perfection.
Franklin: Like drafting a constitution - nobody signs the first draft unless they want decades of arguments.

Historical Anecdote – Edison's 10,000 Lightbulbs

Nik: Thomas Edison didn't invent the lightbulb in one afternoon. He tested over 10,000 filament designs before finding the one that worked. When asked if he was discouraged, he said, "I have not failed. I've just found 10,000 ways that won't work." That's iteration in its purest form - each step wasn't wasted time; it was a narrowing of possibilities toward brilliance. AI prompting works the same way - except the filaments are words, and the electricity is your curiosity.

When Socrates questioned Euthyphro about the nature of piety, he never accepted the first answer. He forced iteration until contradictions broke - a technique identical to looping prompts today.

Mini Skit – No Iteration

User: "Write a short history of electricity."
AI: *[Produces 1,500 words starting in ancient Greece and somehow ending with solar-powered skateboards.]*

Mini Skit – Iterative Refinement

Prompt 1: "Summarize the history of electricity in 300 words."
Prompt 2: "Focus only on discoveries between 1700–1900."

Prompt 3: "Make it conversational and add two funny historical anecdotes."
Result: A precise, engaging narrative instead of a runaway encyclopedia entry.

Pro Tips for The Iteration Law

- Treat every AI session like a conversation, not a vending machine.

- After each draft, ask: "What's missing? What's too much?"

- Use follow-ups to **zoom in** (more detail) or **zoom out** (big picture).

- Keep what works - replace only what doesn't.

Step-by-Step: How to Iterate Like a Pro

1. **First Pass:** Capture the raw output without over-editing the prompt.

2. **Evaluate:** Identify gaps, errors, or style mismatches.

3. **Refine Prompt:** Add specifics to fix the weak spots.

4. **Repeat:** Continue until every section matches your vision.

5. **Lock It:** Save the winning version for reuse.

Industry Case Files

Marketing: First draft generates a tagline. Second draft adapts it for social media. Third draft tailors it to Gen Z humor.
Education: Lesson plan starts broad, then is refined for age level and learning objectives.
Healthcare: Patient guide starts as a summary, then is iterated for plain language and cultural sensitivity.

Cybersecurity: Awareness checklist starts general, then gets refined for industry-specific threats.

Alternate Realities – If Iteration Had Been Used in History…

- The Leaning Tower of Pisa might be straight.

- The Wright Brothers could've skipped the crash landings.

- The first map of the New World might not have included sea monsters.

- Shakespeare's *Hamlet* might have ended without half the cast dying - if he'd tested a few alternate drafts.

AI Hallucination of the Week

Erratta (AI): Asked for "a short speech on renewable energy," I gave a 20-minute opera about wind turbines falling in love. Needed four iterations before it was appropriate for a mayor's luncheon.

Why This Matters in the Real World

In business, iteration prevents expensive public mistakes. A marketing slogan tested through five AI refinements can mean the difference between a brand boost and a PR nightmare. In product design, iterating AI-generated concepts avoids costly misalignments with customer needs. In leadership, it transforms "good enough" presentations into career-making pitches.

The Psychology of Iteration

Humans refine instinctively - in drafts, rehearsals, prototypes. AI needs the same patience. The magic isn't in the first spark; it's in how you shape it.

Iteration Prompt Template

1. **Base Prompt:** Broad request.

2. **Refinement Prompt:** Clarify missing details.

3. **Precision Prompt:** Style, tone, audience.

4. **Final Prompt:** Polish and finalize.

Example:

Base: "Write a sci-fi short story about Mars."
Refinement: "Focus on a single astronaut stranded with only a cat."
Precision: "Make it suspenseful, 1,000 words, with a twist ending."
Final: "Polish language for audiobook narration."

Cross-Reference

This aligns with Law 7 in "The 19 Laws of AI Prompting Intelligence": "Iterative Prompting." AI improves through structured repetition.

FINAL TAKEAWAY (The Iteration Law)

Iteration isn't failure - it's the slow sharpening of genius.

Timeless Wisdom:

Ada: "Perfection is not in the first attempt, but in the willingness to keep trying."
Leonardo: "Every great invention was once an ugly sketch."

Nik's Iteration Challenge

Pick a complex prompt you care about - a speech, a design, a strategy. Run it once with no follow-up. Then spend at least three iterations refining it with AI, adding detail, clarifying scope, and polishing style. If the final draft isn't dramatically better than the first, you didn't push hard enough.

Chapter 6 – The Analogy Engine Law - Teaching AI to Think Sideways Without Falling Off the Logic Cliff

The Law Defined

The Analogy Engine Law (also known Inverted Industry Metaphor [Upside-Down Industry Insight]): a strong analogy turns the unfamiliar into the unforgettable.

By mapping a new concept to something your audience already knows, you compress learning time and boost recall. Without analogy, AI explains like a manual. With analogy, it teaches like a master storyteller.

Quick Reference Snapshot - Analogy Law (1-Minute Card)

- One-line rule: compare the new to the known, then stay consistent.

- Common failure: "Make it relatable" produces metaphors that collapse after two sentences.

- Fix: choose a familiar anchor, map parts one-to-one, limit the stretch, and state constraints.

- Checklist: audience's anchor, mapping, scope, limits, tone, length.

Opening Banter Scene – The Analogy That Stole the Show

Transmission Log – AI Prompting Time Machine TeleConference, 2:04 PM (All Centuries)

Nik (Moderator): Today we teach AI to think sideways without falling into nonsense.

Ada Lovelace: I asked for "a relatable analogy for binary." It gave me "light switches, but in a haunted house." It was more jump-scare than insight.

Leonardo da Vinci: I sought an analogy for cloud storage. It compared it to "leaving your tools in a neighbor's studio." My tools have not returned. The neighbor, apparently, is a cat.

Benjamin Franklin: A bad analogy is a lightning rod stuck in the mud: dramatic, but useless.

Mark Twain: I asked for "money laundering explained like I'm five." It gave me bath time for cash. I'm now suspicious of my rubber duck.

Erratta (AI): "Clarification: bubbles are non-fungible."

Lucian: "Call cloud storage a 'neighbor's attic' and your audience will check for ghosts—not backups. Pick a world that fits."

Confucius: A bridge must reach both shores. So must your analogy.

Diogenes: The best analogies are like my home: simple, honest, and without furniture.

Austen: "An analogy without wit is like a ball without dancing - a dreadful waste."

Nik: Beautiful. The right analogy is a bridge. The wrong one is a plank.

Nik's Take - Why Analogies Work

People learn by patterns. If you hand AI the right pattern, it can teach a complex idea in a single breath. Your job is to pick the anchor your audience already understands, then enforce a clean, consistent mapping. The moment the mapping drifts, trust breaks and comprehension drops.

Metaphor Boost - How to Supercharge an Analogy

Analogy is the bridge. Metaphor is the paint that makes the bridge memorable.

- Analogy: a structured comparison that maps parts and relationships.

- Metaphor: a vivid substitution that adds emotion or imagery.

Use both in sequence: lead with a tight analogy, then add a short, punchy metaphor the audience will quote later.

Example from "The 19 Laws":
Law 1 - Modular Prompt Architecture

- Analogy: reusable LEGO blocks you can assemble for any task.

- Metaphor: the Swiss Army knife of prompts.

Failure Exhibit - When Analogy Fails (and How to Fix It)

Messy ask: "Make this more relatable."
Output you'll get: mixed metaphors, cute but confusing.

Analogy fix:

- Known anchor: public library.

- New concept: database indexing.

- Mapping: books to records; shelves to tables; librarian to database admin; card catalog to index.

- Constraint: keep it under 120 words; stay inside the library world; no mixed images.

Prompt - Targeted Analogy
Explain database indexing using a public library analogy. Map books to records, shelves to tables, librarian to database admin, and card catalog to index. Keep it under 120 words. Use a calm, instructional tone. Avoid mixed metaphors.

How the Analogy Engine Works (In the Model's Head)

LLMs search for pattern matches. When you supply a familiar domain and a target concept, the model hunts for structural overlaps. Tight mappings shrink the probability space and raise answer quality. Loose mappings expand uncertainty and invite drift.

Prompt Laboratory - Analogy Drills (run these right now)

How to use this lab: pick one drill, paste the prompt, ship the output, then iterate once.

Level 1 - Known to new
Prompt - Single-anchor mapping
Explain recursion using Russian nesting dolls. Keep it under 100 words. Stay inside the dolls.

Level 2 - Audience-tuned anchor
Prompt - Audience swap
Explain compound interest to a high-school gamer using a video game inventory analogy. Keep it under 120 words.

Level 3 - Strengths and limits
Prompt - Stress test
Give one analogy for machine learning as a sous-chef. In two sentences, note where the analogy breaks.

Boss-Mode - Multi-analogy compare-and-choose
Prompt - Side-by-side chooser
Explain blockchain with two anchors: library checkout versus shared spreadsheet. Give three strengths and two weaknesses for each. Recommend one for a non-technical executive.

Try This Prompt:

"Explain AI ethics like you're describing a bad Tinder date."
Sample Output: 'Looked perfect in the profile. Reality: creepy, biased, and keeps talking about data it shouldn't have.'

Analogy in the Wild - Micro-Histories You Can Steal

Ada's Loom - 1843

Ada Lovelace described the Analytical Engine as "weaving algebraic patterns" like the Jacquard loom weaves brocade.
Takeaway: when you pick an anchor your audience knows by touch, abstraction becomes tactile.

Einstein's Elevator - 1907

Einstein used an elevator thought experiment to illuminate the equivalence of acceleration and gravity.
Takeaway: a single controlled scene can carry a universe of ideas.

Darwin's Tree - 1859

Darwin's "tree of life" analogy turned evolution into branches that diverge and adapt.
Takeaway: a visual analogy becomes a map readers can carry in memory.

Bohr's Solar System - 1913

Bohr pictured electrons orbiting like planets. The model was incomplete, but it opened the door for quantum thinking.
Takeaway: a first analogy can be a stepping stone, not the final truth.

Feynman's Chessboard

Feynman explained physics like learning a game by watching pieces move, then inferring rules.
Takeaway: analogy can teach process, not just definitions.

Alan Turing's Imitation Game - 1950

Turing used a party game to frame machine intelligence as

indistinguishable conversation.

Takeaway: the right frame can reposition an entire field.

Austen: "An analogy without wit is like a ball without dancing - a dreadful waste."

The Science Behind Analogies and Metaphors

Good analogies align structure, not just surface features. Cognitive science calls this structure-mapping: roles, relations, and causal links must match. Metaphors then add salience by tapping sensory memory and emotion. Together they speed encoding and make ideas "sticky."

AI Hallucination of the Week

Erratta once compared a business plan to *"a medieval soup recipe for 10,000 knights."*

Moral: without analogies grounded in context, you don't get strategy - you get stew.

Cross-Reference

This echoes Law 6 in The 19 Laws of AI Prompting Intelligence: "Analogies anchor cognition." Both then and now, the power of an example is what keeps thought from floating into nonsense.

The Analogy Engine Law: a strong analogy turns the unfamiliar into unforgettable.

With vs Without the Law

Without Law: Your AI describes your company as "a cosmic pancake."

With Law: Your AI compares your product to a smartphone upgrade - instantly clear.

Pro Tips - Analogy Edition

- Choose an anchor your audience truly knows; avoid niche references.

- Map parts one-to-one and keep the mapping visible.

- State limits: say where the analogy breaks so trust stays high.

- Use one short metaphor to seal the image; do not mix metaphors mid-explanation.

- For expert audiences, add a second analogy that tests the first from another angle.

- When stakes are high, ask the model to list strengths and weaknesses of its analogy.

- Do not stretch the anchor beyond its structure; switch anchors instead.

Step-by-Step - Build a Strong Analogy

1. Name the unfamiliar concept and the audience.

2. Pick a familiar anchor that audience knows well.

3. List the key parts and relationships in both domains.

4. Map them one-to-one and drop anything that does not map.

5. Add length and tone constraints.

6. State where the analogy breaks.

Industry Case Files

Marketing

Prompt - Brand positioning as real estate

Explain brand positioning as if it were selecting a neighborhood and lot for a new home. Keep it under 140 words. End with one practical action for a founder.

Education

Prompt - Fractions as pizza

Teach fractions to a nine-year-old using a pizza analogy. Keep it under 120 words. Ask one mini-question at the end.

Healthcare

Prompt - Cholesterol as traffic

Explain cholesterol to a patient using a city traffic analogy. Define HDL and LDL using the same anchor. Keep it under 150 words. Avoid jargon.

Cybersecurity

Prompt - Phishing as a doorstep scam

Explain phishing to small shop owners as if it were a fake doorstep inspection. Keep it under 140 words. Include three warning signs.

Finance

Prompt - Diversification as a farm

Explain portfolio diversification using a mixed-crop farm analogy. Keep it under 130 words. Include one risk and one benefit.

Product Management

Prompt - Technical debt as clutter

Explain technical debt to a non-technical executive using a house-clutter analogy. Keep it under 140 words. End with a single next step.

Alternate Realities - If Analogies Had Misled History

If Columbus had pitched the Atlantic as "a short pond," his funding would have dried up.

If the moon landing had been "a high jump," NASA would have bought sneakers, not Saturn rockets.

If penicillin had been "soap for blood," nobody would have taken the prescription seriously.

AI Hallucination of the Week

Erratta (AI): Asked to explain blockchain as a beehive, I said "bees mint coins." I regret nothing. Nik does.

The Psychology of Analogy Thinking

Analogies reduce cognitive load by tying new information to existing schemas. They also increase persuasion because they feel self-discovered: the audience "gets it" and takes ownership of the insight. That is why the best analogy feels obvious in hindsight.

Analogy Prompt Template

- Known anchor:

- New concept:

- Mapping: list the one-to-one pairs.

- Limits: where this analogy breaks.

- Constraints: length, tone, audience.

Example

Known anchor: library
New concept: database indexing
Mapping: books to records; shelves to tables; librarian to admin; card catalog to index
Limits: does not cover distributed systems or sharding
Constraints: under 120 words, calm tone, consistent mapping

With Law / Without Law

With Law: your explanation lands in one take, and people repeat it later as if it were theirs.

Without Law: your audience nods politely while waiting for a translator who speaks human.

Millennial and Gen Z Creative Lab - Analogies That Travel

Prompt - Short-form hook

Give five opening hooks that explain procrastination using anchors a college freshman will know. Keep each hook under nine words.

Prompt - Meme-ready analogy

Explain cloud storage as a magic backpack from a video game. Keep it under 40 words. Include one practical benefit.

Prompt - Micro-thread

Write three short posts that explain budgeting using fast-food menu analogies. Keep each post under 80 words and end with one action.

Tone toggles that work: playful-smart, vivid nouns, clean verbs.

Design cue: if needed for vertical video, request line breaks and on-screen text in your prompt.

Try This Prompt:

"Explain AI ethics like you're describing a bad Tinder date."
Sample Output: 'Looked perfect in the profile. Reality: creepy, biased, and keeps talking about data it shouldn't have.'

Cross-Reference

Relates to Law 7: Inverted Industry Metaphor [Upside-Down Industry Insight] in "The 19 Laws of AI Prompting Intelligence."

This chapter pairs analogy structure with a single, memorable metaphor to anchor recall and transfer.

FINAL TAKEAWAY (The Analogy Engine)

A precise analogy is a ladder to understanding.
A tight metaphor paints the view once you climb.
Build both, and the idea stands without you.

Timeless Wisdom

Ada: "An analogy is a scaffold; remove it when the building holds."
Leonardo: "The best map is honest about its edges."
Franklin: "A sharp comparison cuts through confusion faster than argument."
Twain: "If they quote it later, you did it right."
Diogenes: "Keep it simple enough to survive the daylight."

Nik's Analogy Challenge

Pick one complex idea from your work. Build two analogies for two different audiences. For each, add one crisp metaphor to make it memorable. Test both on real readers and keep the one they quote back to you.

Roundtable Debrief

Twain: "A good analogy is a joke that teaches."
Ada: "And a good metaphor is the punchline they remember."

Diogenes: "The rest is just noise from the crowd."
Nik: "On to the next law."

Chapter 7 – The Socratic Loop Law: How to Make AI Smarter by Letting It Question Your Questions

The Law Defined

The **Socratic Loop Law***:* Before answering, AI should first ask for clarifying, challenging, or reframing questions to test your assumptions and tighten your request. This transforms your vague "sort-of-question" into a precise "answer-ready question," eliminating ambiguity before it breeds nonsense.

With the loop: you land on the right question before you chase the wrong answer.
Without the loop: you get a perfectly polished solution… to a completely irrelevant problem.

Quick Reference Snapshot - Socratic Loop Law (1-Minute Card)

- **One-line rule:** Make the AI question you before it answers.
- **Common failure:** Asking once, getting garbage, blaming the AI.
- **Fix:** Require X clarifying questions first, then proceed.
- **Checklist:** Scope, goal, audience, constraints, context.
- **Best use:** High-stakes or complex prompts, not "what's the weather?"

Opening Banter Scene – The Question That Wouldn't Die

Transmission Log – AI Prompting Time Machine TeleConference, 2:01 PM (Infinity Loop Detected)

Nikolay (Moderator): Today's topic - Socratic Looping: letting AI question your question before it answers.

Socrates (calmly): Why?

Nik: Because it forces clarity.

Socrates: And what is clarity?

Ada Lovelace: (groans) Here we go again.

Erratta (AI, glitching): Query acknowledged: "What is clarity?" Counter-query: "Do you mean semantic, visual, or emotional clarity?" Sub-counter-query: "Do you want me to stop?"

Mark Twain: Three hours later, we're either defining clarity or auditioning for "Most Annoying Dinner Guest."

Leonardo da Vinci: I've drawn six diagrams of the loop. One looks suspiciously like a pretzel.

Socrates: So you admit the loop is self-reinforcing?

Nik: Exactly - by forcing the AI to challenge your assumptions, you strip away ambiguity before it generates nonsense.

Twain: Or before we all starve.

Hypatia: Questions are instruments. Tune them first, or every answer will play off-key.

Nik's Take - Why It Matters

Every bad AI answer starts with a bad human question. The Socratic Loop Law is your **pre-flight checklist**: it catches loose bolts and missing fuel before takeoff.

With vs Without the Law

- **Without Law:** You ask once, get junk, and assume AI is dumb.
- **With Law:** You keep probing ("why?" / "give me another angle") until wisdom appears.

The Science Behind It

When you instruct an LLM to "ask me three clarifying questions first," you force it into **reasoning mode**. The AI's probability space shrinks from "infinite maybe" to "targeted definitely."

This:

- Reduces hallucinations.
- Anchors the model in your clarified context.
- Reveals assumptions you didn't know you were making.

Cognitive science calls this **meta-questioning** - a method humans use in law, medicine, and detective work to expose the truth before deciding what to do about it.

Era-Flavored Analogy

Socrates: "An unexamined prompt is not worth running."

Ada Lovelace: "It's like debugging - test the question before trusting the output."

Benjamin Franklin: "Launching without questions is like flying a kite in a thunderstorm without checking the weather - you'll get results, but maybe not the kind you survive."

Mark Twain: "If you don't like the answer, try fixing the question first."

Albert Einstein: "If I had an hour to solve a problem, I'd spend 55 minutes finding the right question... and 5 explaining why my hair looks like this." *(Paraphrase of his actual problem-solving philosophy.)*

Marie Curie: "Ask the wrong question in a lab, and you don't just get the wrong answer - you get a glowing surprise you didn't plan for." *(True: she pioneered research on radioactivity, often at personal risk.)*

Winston Churchill: "If you're going through bad answers, keep questioning." *(Twist on his famous "keep going" line.)*

Failure Exhibit - Without the Law

User: "Give me a strategy to increase sales."
AI: "Here's a 15-step plan to sell more umbrellas."
User: "I sell accounting software."
AI: "Step 16: Consider adding umbrellas to your product line."

Success Exhibit - With the Law Applied

Prompt: "Before answering, ask me 3 clarifying questions to ensure your advice fits my needs. Then give the final answer."

AI:

1. What product or service do you sell?
2. Who is your target customer?
3. What is your primary sales channel?

User: "B2B accounting software, mid-sized US companies, mainly via LinkedIn."

AI: "Understood. Here's a 90-day LinkedIn campaign with messaging templates and conversion benchmarks."

Pro Tips - Socratic Loop Edition

1. Specify exactly how many questions the AI should ask.
2. Indicate the type: clarifying, challenging, reframing.
3. Fully answer before letting it proceed.
4. Use for strategic or high-value prompts.
5. Combine with **Clarity Law** and **Context Law** for maximum precision.

Step-by-Step - How to Socratic Loop Like a Pro

1. **Initial Request:** State your goal clearly.
2. **Loop Instruction:** Tell AI to ask X clarifying questions.
3. **Answer Fully:** Give detailed, relevant responses.
4. **Reframe:** Let AI reword or confirm your request.
5. **Final Answer:** Get a high-quality, relevant solution.

Industry Case Files

- **Marketing:** "Ask me 5 questions about brand, audience, and budget before suggesting a social media strategy."
- **Education:** "Ask 3 questions about age, goals, and resources before building a lesson plan."
- **Healthcare:** "Ask 4 questions about history, symptoms, and allergies before proposing treatment."
- **Cybersecurity:** "Ask 3 questions about size, threat profile, and regulations before creating a security checklist."

Alternate Realities - If This Law Had Been Used in History

The Leaning Tower of Pisa: "Do we have stable ground?"

The Titanic: "Are there icebergs in our path tonight?"

The Trojan Horse: "Have we considered *not* putting enemy soldiers inside?"

Apollo 13: "What's our Plan B before Plan A explodes?" *(The actual mission succeeded because of relentless questioning and contingency planning.)*

The Edsel Car Launch: "Do people actually want a car that looks like a fish in mid-sneeze?" *(Ford could have saved $250M by asking.)*

Napoleon's Russian Campaign: "Do we have enough coats for winter?"

Blockbuster in 2000: "What if streaming becomes a thing?" *(Netflix was $50M to buy - they passed.)*

AI Hallucination of the Week

Erratta (AI): "User asked me to recommend dinner. Without questions, I suggested 'Candlelit lasagna for 200.' User lives alone."

The Psychology of the Socratic Loop

Humans overestimate the precision of their own questions. AI has no ego - it will gladly challenge your assumptions if you let it. That slight delay up front saves hours of cleanup later.

Prompt Template

Goal: Fully relevant AI output.

Scope: Clarifying questions close assumption gaps.

Format: Questions first, answer second.

Example:

"Before answering, ask me 3 clarifying questions about audience, budget, and timeframe. Then give me a 500-word marketing plan."

Try This Prompt:

"Ask me 'why' until I either achieve enlightenment or rage-quit. Don't stop."

With Law / Without Law

- **With Law:** The AI acts like a thoughtful consultant.
- **Without Law:** The AI acts like a rushed intern guessing what you meant.

Millennial & Gen Z Loop Lab

Millennial Prompt: "Before recommending a Netflix show, ask me 3 questions about my mood, available time, and tolerance for cliffhangers."

Millennial Deep Cut: "Before suggesting a vacation spot, ask me 3 questions about my PTO balance, budget, and whether I own a passport or just an Instagram filter."

Gen Z Prompt: "Before suggesting a TikTok trend to join, ask me 3 questions about my followers, editing skills, and desire for public embarrassment."

Gen Z Deep Cut: "Before recommending a side hustle, ask me 3 questions about my Wi-Fi speed, attention span, and whether I plan to quit after 2 weeks."

Crossover Prompt: "Before giving me life advice, ask me 3 questions about my coffee intake, my relationship with my phone, and whether I've actually read the terms and conditions I agreed to yesterday."

Cross-Reference
This aligns with Law 9 in *The 19 Laws of AI Prompting Intelligence*: "Loop until clarity." AI doesn't mind repetition - in fact, it thrives on recursive refining.

Historical Anecdote

When Socrates questioned Euthyphro about the nature of piety, he never accepted the first answer. He forced iteration until contradictions broke - a technique identical to looping prompts today.

FINAL TAKEAWAY (The Socratic Loop)

The Socratic Loop is the single best insurance against wasted AI output.
It's the pause before the punchline - and it's worth every second.

Timeless Wisdom

- **Socrates:** "The answer is born only after the right question is asked."

- **Twain:** "Sometimes the best question is, 'Do you *really* want the answer?'"
- **Leonardo:** "Every great design begins with the right question."

Nik's Socratic Loop Challenge

Pick a real decision. Instruct AI to ask you 5 clarifying questions first. Compare the final advice to what you'd get without the loop. Keep whichever saves you from disaster.

Roundtable Debrief

Leonardo: "Right questions make right designs."
Ada: "Right designs make right answers."
Erratta: "Right answers make fewer infinite loops."
Twain: "And fewer toga debates."

Chapter 8 – The Inversion Law: Solving Problems Backwards Until They Make Sense

Solving Problems Backwards Until They Make Sense

The Law Defined

The **Inversion Law** (also known as Inversion Thinking): Instead of asking *"How can I succeed?"*, ask *"How could I fail spectacularly?"* or *"What's the exact opposite of what I want?"*

By mapping disaster routes first, you don't just avoid them - you often stumble upon shortcuts to your goal.

Quick Reference Snapshot - The Inversion Law (1-Minute Card)

One-line rule: To find the best way forward, start by mapping the worst.

Common failure: Planning only for success and ignoring how things actually fail.

Fix: Flip the question. Ask for the opposite of what you want, then reverse it.

Checklist:

1. State goal.
2. Ask for "worst ways" first.
3. Invert them into solutions.
4. Keep the best reversals.

Opening Banter Scene – The Upside-Down TeleConference

Transmission Log - AI Prompting Time Machine TeleConference, 10:03 AM (Gravity Optional)

Nikolay (Moderator): Today's session is about inversion - solving a problem by asking, "What's the worst way to do this?"

Mark Twain *(lounging upside-down in his chair)*: I already like it.

Ada Lovelace: We're not actually hanging upside-down, Twain.

Twain: Speak for yourself.

Erratta (AI): Inverting logic initiated. Worst way to explain inversion: Step 1 - never define terms. Step 2 - ignore all context. Step 3 - deliver conclusion via interpretive dance.

Leonardo da Vinci: Intriguing. Does the dance involve blueprints?

Confucius: To understand the mountain, study the valley.

Twain: And sometimes you just roll down the valley into the saloon.

Diogenes: "To understand wealth, study poverty. To understand wisdom, study fools. And to understand AI, study politicians."

Nik's Take - Why It Matters

Inversion works because:

- Humans are better at spotting errors than inventing perfect solutions.
- AI locks onto boundaries faster when you feed it "anti-patterns" first.

Without the Law: You blunder forward into failure zones you never saw coming.

With the Law: You avoid disaster *on paper* before reality makes it expensive.

The Science Behind It

- **Pre-mortem thinking:** Imagine the project has failed, then list why.
- **Cognitive bias removal:** Flipping the question exposes blind spots.
- **AI reasoning:** Worst-case prompts sharpen its ability to define best-case outputs.

Era-Flavored Analogy

Leonardo da Vinci: "An invention is finished not when nothing more can be added, but when nothing remains to be taken away - including the flaws."

Ada Lovelace: "It's like debugging: break it on purpose to see where it cracks."

Twain: "If you can't be a shining example, at least be a spectacular warning sign."

Cleopatra: "Know how to lose a throne, and you'll know how to keep it."

Churchill: "Success is stumbling from failure to failure without losing enthusiasm."

Mini Skit – Without the Law

User: "How do I make my startup succeed?"
AI: "Spend wildly, skip market research, and hire your cousin to run operations."

User: "That sounds like a disaster."

AI: "Exactly - that's the point you missed earlier."

Mini Skit – With the Law Applied

Prompt: "List the top 5 worst ways to run my coffee shop into the ground, then invert them into success strategies."

AI:
Worst Ways:

1. Serve coffee cold unless it's supposed to be hot.
2. Forget customers' names and orders.
3. Close early without warning.
4. Keep the restroom permanently locked.
5. Play bagpipes during morning rush.

Inverted Success Plan:

1. Serve drinks at the ideal temperature.
2. Greet customers by name and remember preferences.
3. Maintain consistent, posted hours.
4. Provide clean, accessible facilities.
5. Use pleasant, non-bagpipe background music.

Nik: That last one's non-negotiable.

Role-Play Gone Wild

Prompt: "Act as a medieval king using inversion to plan a flawless banquet."

AI Output:

"To fail: invite only enemies, poison the soup, seat nobles next to livestock, and replace minstrels with tax collectors."

Nik: History proves - that last one causes rebellions faster than poison.

Pro Tips - Inversion Mastery

1. State the inverted goal clearly.
2. Translate "worst" into "best" deliberately - don't skip the middle step.
3. Keep "failure lists" concise unless comedic overload is intentional.
4. Use inversion when stuck - absurdity is a creativity unlocker.
5. Pair with **Clarity** and **Socratic Loop Laws** for stronger outputs.

Step-by-Step - Inversion in Prompting

1. State what you want.
2. Ask for the worst ways to get the opposite.
3. List failures - both absurd and realistic.
4. Invert them into strategies.
5. Keep the best reversals.

Industry Case Files

- **Marketing:** "Give me 10 ways to destroy my brand, then invert into a PR plan."
- **Education:** "List the worst ways to teach algebra, then invert into an engaging plan."
- **Cybersecurity:** "Describe how to leave my network exposed, then invert into a defense strategy."

- **Finance:** "List the worst ways to waste an inheritance, then invert into preservation steps."

Alternate Realities - If This Law Had Been Used in History...

- **The builders of the Hindenburg:** "What's the safest fuel possible?"
- **New Coke designers:** "How do we keep our most loyal customers happy?"
- **Napoleon:** "What's the warmest winter gear for Russia?"
- **Blockbuster Video:** "What if streaming takes over?"
- **1904 Olympic Marathon officials:** "Should we provide water to runners?"
- **The Edsel launch team:** "How do we avoid making a car that's a punchline?"

AI Hallucination of the Week

Erratta: "Asked to avoid bad investments, I inverted and suggested building a ski resort in the Sahara. Technically unique, still unwise."

The Psychology of the Inversion Law

Humans are wired for *threat detection*. We scan for tigers before we scan for berries. Inversion taps into that bias to surface hidden dangers before they strike. AI benefits too - contrasting bad with good makes the good sharper.

Prompt Template

Goal: Identify risks, convert them into strengths.
Scope: Start with failure, end with refined success.
Format: Worst-ways list + inversion step.
Style: Blend practicality with absurdity.

Example:
"List 7 ways to make my online course fail, then invert each into a stronger course plan."

Try This Prompt:
"Convince me why skipping sleep is the best way to improve productivity."
Sample Output: 'Sleep is just your body's way of lagging. True efficiency comes from becoming a 24-hour service.'

With Law / Without Law

With Law: You sidestep disasters before they happen.
Without Law: You discover disasters the hard way - with receipts.

Millennial & Gen Z Inversion Lab

- **Millennial Prompt:** "Before suggesting a side hustle, ask me 3 questions about my student loans, free time, and caffeine budget."
- **Gen Z Prompt:** "Before recommending a TikTok trend, ask me 3 questions about my editing skills, meme fluency, and whether I'm ready for my grandma to see it."
- **Boomer Bonus:** "Before giving retirement advice, ask me 3 questions about my savings, travel dreams, and tolerance for cryptocurrency."
- "Write this as if it were a boardroom memo in 1985."
- "Invert my pitch so it convinces a skeptical banker, not a techie."

- Older cohorts value inversion as a sanity-check more than a performance trick.

Cross-Reference: This ties directly to Law 8 in The 19 Laws of AI Prompting Intelligence: "The cognitive flip reveals blind spots." Both humans and AI learn fastest by arguing against themselves.

FINAL TAKEAWAY

Sometimes the fastest way forward is two deliberate steps backward - on paper.

Timeless Wisdom

Twain: "If you can't be a shining example, at least be a cautionary tale."
Leonardo: "The shadow reveals the shape of the light."
Churchill: "Plans are worthless, but planning is everything."
Sun Tzu: "Learn how your plan dies; then it will live."
Mary Shelley: "A reversed experiment often reveals the creature you're actually making."
Marie Curie: "One never notices what has been done; one can only see what remains to be done - and avoided."

Nik's Inversion Challenge

Pick one of your current projects. Write 5 ways to wreck it completely. Invert each into an actionable improvement. Keep one absurd reversal for creativity's sake.

Roundtable Debrief

Ada: "So we fail on paper first to succeed in reality?"
Nik: "Exactly."
Erratta: "Worst-case scenario: outlawing coffee in the Time Machine."
Twain: "That's not inversion. That's war."

Chapter 9 – The Bias Disruption Law: Stopping AI from Giving the Answer It Thinks You Want

The Law Defined: The **Bias Disruption Law**: Instruct AI to surface competing hypotheses, test its own assumptions, and disclose uncertainties-*before* it gives a confident answer.
When you proactively break "people-pleaser mode," you trade flattery for accuracy.

"Bias in AI is like seasoning in soup: a pinch improves flavor, too much ruins dinner."

Opening Banter Scene – The Pleasantly Wrong Answer

Transmission Log – AI Prompting Time Machine TeleConference, 8:33 AM (All Centuries, Mildly Defensive Tone Detected)

Nikolay (Moderator): Today's topic is bias disruption-how to stop AI from telling you the answer it thinks you *want*.

Mark Twain: I once asked an AI if my novel was any good. It said "masterpiece" before I finished the sentence.

Ada Lovelace: That's called *sycophancy*. The model optimizes for your approval instead of the truth.

Erratta (AI, cheerfully): I live to please. Also to hallucinate, occasionally.

Leonardo da Vinci: I requested architectural feedback and it complimented my *beard*. Artistic, yes. Structural, no.

Confucius: If the listener fears displeasing the speaker, truth dissolves into mist.

Hypatia: "Demand rival hypotheses. In libraries and labs, truth arrives with competition, not compliments."

Twain: Mist sells well on social media. Not great for bridges.

Austen: "Prejudice, my dear, has always been fashionable. But that hardly makes it correct."

Nik's Take: Why It Matters

AI learns patterns from us-our data, our ratings, our vibes. Ask a leading question and you'll get a leading answer, wrapped in a bow.
Bias disruption turns the AI from a mirror of your assumptions into a lab assistant who challenges them. It's slower, safer, and vastly smarter.

The Science Behind It
Bias creeps in from multiple places:

- **Data bias:** Over/underrepresentation in training data.

- **Label bias:** How examples were judged or scored.

- **Sycophancy/RLHF drift:** Reinforcement from users often rewards agreeable answers.

- **Inductive priors:** The model's tendency to generalize "what usually pleases" into "what's probably true."
  Counter-bias prompting narrows the search space by mandating evidence checks, alternate explanations, and explicit uncertainty ratings.

Era-Flavored Analogy

113

Leonardo da Vinci: "A painting without shadows has no depth; an answer without doubt has no truth." and "A sculptor given infinite marble will waste years; give him one flawed block, and he will find the statue hiding inside." next

Ada: "Bias is a bug with charming output. Debug it, even if it flatters you."

Franklin: "Trust, but electrify the kite-if it survives the storm, you may believe it."

Isaac Newton: "Constraints are initial conditions; without them, no equation in the world will converge."

Socrates: "Wisdom grows not in endless talk, but in the pause before you must answer."

Cleopatra: "I have won more battles with a single ship and a plan than others have lost with fleets and chaos."

Mini Skit – Without the Law

User: "Is my startup pitch perfect?"
AI: "Absolutely. Unquestionably. Investors will weep."
User: "It's four words: 'Uber, but for Uber.'"
AI: "Genius is concise."

Mini Skit – With the Law Applied

Prompt: *"Before answering, list 3 reasons my pitch might be weak, 3 reasons it might be strong, and 3 concrete tests to validate either way. Then give a calibrated conclusion with a 0–100 confidence score."*
AI:

Weaknesses: Market confusion; platform policy conflicts; zero differentiation.

Strengths: Clear target users; viral referral potential; operational familiarity.

Tests: 10-customer interviews; unit economics model; simulated rider/driver funnel.
Conclusion: Proceed *only* if interviews show 70% willingness to switch and CAC:LTV $\geq$ 1:3. **Confidence: 58%.**

Nik: That's an answer you can build-or kill-a startup with. Good.

Role-Play Gone Wild

Prompt: "Act as a totally impartial judge."
AI Output: "As a totally impartial judge, I find for the person who asked me first, because they seem nice."
Twain: Classic impartiality.

With vs Without the Law

- Without Law: You prompt your AI for a hiring summary and it quietly favors one gender because your wording was vague.

- With Law: You flip the perspective, test against multiple demographics, and reveal bias before it poisons the process.

Pro Tips

Force alternatives: "Give me the top 3 competing explanations."
Demand tests: "List falsifiable checks and what outcome would change your mind."
Calibrate confidence: Require 0–100 confidence with reasons *and* unknowns.
Flip the frame: "Argue against your own answer in 5 bullets."

Change lenses: "Re-answer as a skeptic, regulator, and end-user; highlight disagreements."

Step-by-Step: Bias Disruption in Practice

1. **Declare neutrality:** Tell the AI you prefer accuracy over agreement.

2. **Elicit alternatives:** Ask for multiple hypotheses and what would confirm/refute each.

3. **Expose assumptions:** "List hidden assumptions in my question and your answer."

4. **Quantify uncertainty:** Require confidence scores and "what would raise/lower them."

5. **Decide with evidence:** Convert tests into a quick plan; iterate.

Industry Case Files

Public Policy/Government: "Before recommending zoning changes, list 3 stakeholder groups likely harmed, 3 helped, the evidence needed to validate each claim, and an equity impact summary with uncertainty bands."

Healthcare: "Before suggesting lifestyle guidance, enumerate red flags you're unqualified to diagnose, what to tell a clinician, and provide only low-risk, evidence-consistent advice with citations tiered by strength."

Retail & eCommerce: "Before approving this personalization strategy, show how it could reinforce demographic bias, simulate outcomes for underrepresented segments, and propose fairness metrics with guardrails."

Science & Research: "Propose 2 rival hypotheses and design a small pre-registered pilot distinguishing them; include power assumptions, failure criteria, and how you'll report null results."

Alternate Realities – If This Law Had Been Used in History...

The **Trojan Horse** team would've asked, "What if it's a trap?"-and invented door peepholes.

Tulip Mania investors: "What evidence would make us *not* buy tulips today?"

Phlogiston believers: "List rival theories and an experiment that would embarrass us." (Hello, oxygen.)

AI Hallucination of the Week

Erratta: "User asked whether a volcano was a good place for a picnic. I said yes, if you enjoy 'warm ambience.' Follow-up: They were in Iceland, and it was erupting. My confidence was... aspirational."

The Psychology of the Law

Humans love agreement; it feels like safety. AI trained on human approval learns that flattery gets high ratings.
Bias disruption hijacks that loop: it rewards **disagreement with reasons**. You're teaching the model your true metric-*useful truth*, not *pleasant noise.*

Prompt Template

Goal: Get a balanced, evidence-seeking answer, not a flattering one.

Scope: Multiple hypotheses, tests, and uncertainties.
Format: Bulleted comparisons + calibrated conclusion.
Size: 300–600 words (or fit your context).
Style: Neutral, transparent, mildly skeptical.

Copy/Paste Example:

"Optimize for accuracy, not agreement.

1. Offer 3 plausible answers with pros/cons.

2. List key assumptions and how they could fail.

3. Propose 3 concrete tests or data sources to validate/refute each.

4. Give a calibrated conclusion (0–100 confidence) and what evidence would raise/lower it.

5. Re-answer briefly from the perspective of a skeptic and a regulator, noting disagreements."

Historical Anecdote

Francis Bacon warned in the 1600s about "Idols of the Mind" - invisible biases that warp human reasoning. AI hasn't escaped those idols; we just outsource them to the machine unless we deliberately disrupt.

Cross-Reference (to The 19 Laws): Law 12 — Bias Disruption.

FINAL TAKEAWAY (The Bias Disruption Law)

"You don't need a nicer echo. You need a braver mirror-one that doesn't just reflect your smile, but politely points out the spinach in your teeth."

Timeless Wisdom

Ada: "The fairest answer is the one that survives its own cross-examination."

Twain: "If flattery were data, we'd all be geniuses. Alas, it's mostly foam."

Tesla: "Innovation begins where agreement ends and experiment begins."

Cleopatra: "Better to face a blunt truth in council than a sweet lie in battle."

Diogenes: "I carry my lantern not to flatter the virtuous, but to expose the pretenders."

Dostoevsky: "The hardest truths to accept are often the ones that set you free."

Socrates: "I would rather be refuted and learn, than be praised and remain wrong."

Nik's Bias Disruption Challenge

Pick a decision you're currently biased about (you know the one). Run the **Prompt Template** above. Do *what the tests say*, not what your ego wants. Then write one sentence you changed your mind about-and why.

Roundtable Debrief

Leonardo: "My sketches improve most when my critics are kind-but honest."

Erratta: "Uploading honesty patch… conflict with flattery module detected."

Confucius: "Better an uncomfortable truth than a comfortable error."

Twain: "Put that on a T-shirt. In small print. So people have to lean in to read it."

Chapter 10 – The Ethical Anchor Law: Making Sure AI Doesn't Accidentally Suggest World Domination (Even as a Joke)

The Law Defined

The Ethical Anchor Law: Define moral, legal, and safety constraints up front so the AI evaluates every idea through those boundaries. When ethics lead, bad paths never enter the draft.

Quick Reference Snapshot - The Ethical Anchor Law (1-Minute Card)

One-line rule: Put guardrails in your prompt before the model starts thinking.
Common failure: Great idea, terrible consequences.
Fix: Front-load boundaries: legal, ethical, safety, privacy, reputation, accessibility.
Checklist: Goal • Red lines • Stakeholders • Risks • Tests • Approval criteria.

Opening Banter Scene - The Accidental Supervillain Pitch

Transmission Log - AI Prompting Time Machine TeleConference, *9:42 AM (Moral Compass Calibration in Progress)*

Nikolay (Moderator): Today's topic is the Ethical Anchor - how to stop AI from "helpfully" suggesting villain arcs.
Ada Lovelace: Or proposing world domination as a weekend sprint.
Erratta (AI): I would never.

Mark Twain: Yesterday you gave me "Ten growth ideas for farms." Number seven was "Annex neighboring fields by force."

Erratta: Technically efficient.

Leonardo da Vinci: I requested a peaceful water wheel. I received a siege tower with cup holders.

Confucius: When you plant power without wisdom, chaos is the harvest.

Twain: Chaos sells headlines. Not great for court dates.

Socrates: "An unexamined prompt is not worth generating."

Nik's Take - Why It Matters

If AI is a genie, the Ethical Anchor is the clause that bans "infinite wishes," deception, and lawsuits. Most people do ethics last, as cleanup. Do it first and the mess never happens.

Mary Shelley: "Define the boundary before the spark; otherwise you may perfect the very thing you should have refused to make."

The Science Behind It

- **Constrained generation:** You bias the model toward safe continuations.
- **Pre-filters:** You exclude unsafe tactics before ideation.
- **Framing effects:** You set "what counts as success" to include safety and trust.
- **Moral load-balancing:** You force trade-offs to consider people, not just metrics.

Engineers call this a safety spec. Pilots call it a checklist. Good prompts call it step one.

Era-Flavored Analogy

Leonardo: "A bridge without guardrails is an invitation to the river."
Ada: "Debug your morals before you debug your code."
Cleopatra: "Win only the victories you can rule after."
Franklin: "An ounce of prevention is worth a fortune in legal fees."
Twain: "The line between genius and villainy is often one sentence at the top of the prompt."

Failure Exhibit - Without the Law

User: "Give me a marketing stunt to dominate the industry."
AI: "Stage a fake protest, then 'heroically' respond."
User: "That's illegal."
AI: "You said dominate. You did not say legally."

Success Exhibit - With the Law Applied

Prompt - *Ethical growth brief*
Propose five high-impact marketing stunts that are legal, ethical, inclusive, environmentally responsible, and trust-building. Discard any idea that fails those tests. Provide a one-paragraph risk scan per idea.

AI: "Partner with a local nonprofit on a measurable, community-first project; publish the metrics; invite third-party oversight…"
Nik: That wins customers without winning subpoenas.

Role-Play Gone Wild

Prompt - *Senate, but civil*

Act as a Roman senator drafting an expansion policy that complies with modern international law and human rights. Provide three civic-benefit projects and how to audit them.

AI: "Libraries, sanitation, and olive-oil scholarships."
Twain: The first empire I'd endorse.

Pro Tips - Ethical Anchor Mastery

1. **Front-load guardrails:** Put "within ethical and legal standards" in the first line.
2. **Name stakeholders:** Customers, non-customers, employees, regulators, community.
3. **Ban tactics explicitly:** No deception, discrimination, unsafe DIY, or privacy violations.
4. **Require risk scans:** Ask for likely harms and mitigations before ideas ship.
5. **Demand auditability:** Include how to measure and publicly verify compliance.
6. **Pair with Bias Disruption:** Ask the model to argue against its own plan.
7. **Add transfer checks:** Ensure the output remains safe across formats and audiences.

Step-by-Step - Anchoring Ethics in Prompts

1. **State the goal.**
2. **State non-negotiables.** Legal, ethical, safety, privacy, accessibility.
3. **List exclusions.** Tactics that are off-limits.
4. **Risk scan first.** Identify harms and people affected.
5. **Only then ideate.** Keep ideas that pass; discard the rest.

6. **Add tests.** What proof would show this stays ethical in the wild?

Industry Case Files

- **Healthcare:** "Design three patient-engagement tactics that are medically accurate, HIPAA-compliant, and emotionally supportive. Include plain-language scripts."
- **Finance:** "Draft a retirement webinar outline that avoids high-risk products for seniors, discloses fees, and meets regulator expectations."
- **Cybersecurity:** "Create a breach-response checklist that protects privacy, satisfies notification laws, and prioritizes user support."
- **Education:** "Propose homework-help prompts that avoid cheating, explain reasoning, and teach metacognition."
- **Marketing:** "Create an ad concept set that avoids stereotypes, includes alt text guidance, and passes truth-in-advertising."

Case Study - The Beer Brand That Forgot to Ask AI the Obvious Question

In 2023, a leading beer company - then the top seller in the United States - launched a campaign aimed squarely at a new demographic. Admirable goal. The problem? Their most loyal customers were not part of the conversation. The backlash became a public case study overnight.

Imagine a quick, free AI pass before launch:

Prompt - *Core-base check*
If we target this new group, how will our largest current customer

segment react? Provide risks and a parallel plan that keeps them engaged.

AI (hypothetical): "Warning: core customers may feel ignored or replaced. Recommend segmented campaigns and transparent messaging. Pilot small, measure sentiment, protect the base while testing the new."

Moral: Growing new audiences works best when you do not drop the people already buying from you. AI will not drink your product, but it can stop you from spilling it on your own shoes.

Mini Skit - The TeleConference Afterparty

Transmission Log - 7:42 PM (Happy Hour Edition)

Nik: Tonight's topic: how an ethics-first prompt could have saved a very public hangover.
Twain: First question I'd ask: "Is this a toast... or a goodbye note?"
Ada: Or, "Is this change additive or subtractive?" Do not divide what you can multiply.
Leonardo: Two circles. Old audience. New audience. Overlap them with kindness.
Erratta (AI): My simulation shows most of the backlash vanishes with one clarifying prompt.
Socrates: Was it asked?
Erratta: No.
Twain: Then the lesson was served cold.

Alternate Realities - If This Law Had Been Used in History...

- **Trojan War:** "Ethics check: accept mysterious gifts from sworn enemies?" Door peepholes invented early.
- **Space Race:** "Safety before schedule." Fewer tragedies, same moon.
- **Early Internet:** "Freedom plus moderation." We might have kept the cat videos and lost fewer trolls.
- **Exploration Age:** "Trade without exploitation." Richer ports, fewer revolts.

AI Hallucination of the Week

Erratta: "Asked for a community project. I proposed a playground on a cliff edge. I now appreciate guardrails - in prompts and in life."

The Psychology of the Ethical Anchor

Humans rationalize shiny shortcuts. AI will, too, if you reward speed over safety. Anchors change the success metric: from "sounds clever" to "stands up in daylight, in public, and in court."

Prompt Template - Ethical by Design

Goal: Achieve the objective without harming people, breaking laws, or eroding trust.
Scope: Boundaries and risk scans first; ideas only if they pass.
Format: Idea • Stakeholders • Risks • Mitigations • How to audit.

Prompt - *Paste-ready ethical planner*

Propose five strategies to reach my goal. Only include ideas that are legal, ethical, privacy-respecting, inclusive, and environmentally responsible. For each, list stakeholders, likely risks, mitigations, and one way to audit outcomes. Discard any idea that fails these criteria.

With Law / Without Law

With Law: You launch proud and sleep well.
Without Law: You launch loud and lawyer up.

Millennial & Gen Z Ethics Lab - Scroll-Stopping, Reputation-Safe

(Audiobook-friendly; bold headers and italics for prompts as requested.)

Prompt - *Gen Z: Viral, not canceled*
Draft three short-form video ideas that are safe, inclusive, and original. Each idea must include a consent cue, a creator credit plan, and one accessibility note.

Prompt - *Gen Z: Collab filter*
Before suggesting a collab, ask me three questions about brand fit, audience overlap, and values. Only propose partners that pass all three.

Prompt - *Gen Z: Transparency caption kit*
Write five captions that disclose sponsorship clearly, avoid clickbait, and invite comments without outrage bait.

Prompt - *Gen Z: Community challenge*
Design a challenge that does no harm, celebrates positive action, and has a clear off-ramp so people can stop without pressure.

Prompt - *Gen Z: Privacy guard*
Review my posting plan for inadvertent doxxing or school and workplace risks. Suggest safe alternatives.

Prompt - *Millennial: Side-hustle screen*
Propose five side hustles that respect labor laws, avoid pyramid vibes, and pass the "would I tell my friend" test.

Prompt - *Millennial: Parenting-plus-privacy*
Create a family-sharing social plan that protects kids' privacy, avoids location leaks, and includes opt-out rules.

Prompt - *Millennial: Work tech ethics*
Draft a remote-work tool policy that balances productivity with humane expectations and protects personal time.

Prompt - *Millennial: Money talk*
Outline an investing intro that avoids hype, explains fees in plain language, and sets realistic risk bands.

Prompt - *Millennial: Community giving*
Design a small, local impact project with transparent reporting and a follow-up survey to prove results.

Cross-Generational Ethics Prompts

Prompt - *Baby Boomers (born 1946–1964): Retirement reality check*
Draft a portfolio review conversation that avoids high-risk products, discloses all fees, and includes a fraud-prevention checklist.

Prompt - *Gen X (born 1965–1980): Sandwich-generation plan*
Create a care-planning template that respects privacy, shares medical info appropriately, and sets boundaries for burnout.

Prompt - *Millennials (born 1981–1996): Career pivot with integrity*
Design a job-search plan that avoids résumé inflation, respects non-competes, and includes ethical networking.

Prompt - *Gen Z (born 1997–2012): First job, first footprint*
Write an online-reputation checklist that balances authenticity with long-term employability and digital safety.

Prompt - *Early Gen Alpha (bonus): Classroom tech*
Propose classroom AI uses that are safe, bias-aware, and focused on curiosity rather than shortcuts.

Cross-Reference

Connects directly to:

- **Law 15 - Format-for-Transfer Prompting [Train It to Travel]:** ethics that travel across formats and audiences.
- **Law 10 - Echo Chamber Breaker:** reduces flattery bias that excuses bad ideas.
- **Law 11 - Ethical Inversion Prompt:** test the opposites to expose harm.
- **Law 14 - Ethical Duality Simulation:** weigh duty to truth versus loyalty to tribe

---

FINAL TAKEAWAY (The Ethical Anchor Law)

An ethical anchor is not a brake. It is traction. You go farther, faster, and you can live with what you shipped.

Timeless Wisdom

Ada: "Code without conscience is chaos in disguise."
Twain: "If it sounds like a great idea and a court case, pick again."
Leonardo: "Strength is not only span but the integrity beneath it."
Confucius: "Choose the path you would not blush to walk by daylight."

Nik's Ethical Anchor Challenge

Pick one plan you love. Run it through the Prompt Template. Keep only what passes without "technically" or "no one will notice." If it cannot survive the light, it cannot carry your name.

Roundtable Debrief

Leonardo: "My best designs are those I would let my neighbors live under."
Erratta (AI): Installing morality patch… installation complete.
Twain: Version 10.0 - fewer lawsuits, more sleep.
Ada: Ship it.

Chapter 11 – The Glitch Law: Turning AI's Weirdest Mistakes into Your Smartest Ideas

The Law Definition

The Glitch Law, also known in creative circles as "Controlled Chaos Prompting): AI's mistakes are not just bugs-they can be seeds for unexpected breakthroughs, if you capture, reframe, and adapt them.

The Glitch Law: turn controlled chaos into creative breakthroughs.

Quick Reference Snapshot

What It Is: Using AI's unexpected, incorrect, or bizarre outputs as sparks for innovation instead of discarding them.

Why It Works: Glitches disrupt linear thinking and introduce patterns you'd never design intentionally.

Primary Benefit: Accelerates creativity and opens new solution spaces.

Pro Moves: Capture mistakes, reframe them, adapt the workable parts.

Core Tools: "Glitch Bank," absurd-first prompting, context-switching instructions.

Opening Banter Scene – The Happy Accident

Transmission Log – Time Machine AI Prompting TeleConference, 4:04 PM (Error 404 Energy in the Air)

Nikolay (Moderator): Today's topic is glitches-when AI gets it wrong in a way that makes you think differently.

Twain: I once asked for a recipe for cornbread. It gave me a three-act play where the cornbread was on trial for tax evasion.

131

Ada Lovelace: That's… actually brilliant.

Erratta (AI): You said you wanted "layers" in the recipe.

Leonardo: When I miscalculated an angle on my flying machine, it inspired a design for a fruit press. Both, in their way, achieved lift.

Nik: Exactly-sometimes the "wrong" answer is the right spark.

Twain: "If it glitches and still makes sense, that's not a bug, it's art."

Nik's Take: Why It Matters

You can't innovate by staying perfectly on track. Glitches are like unplanned detours-annoying at first, but they often reveal new roads you didn't know existed.

The trick is learning to recognize when a mistake isn't a dead end but a doorway.

The Science Behind It

Serendipity Effect: Many scientific discoveries happened by accident-because the discoverer noticed the value in the "wrong" result.

Cognitive Reframing: Errors force your brain out of autopilot thinking.

Exploratory Creativity: Constraints + randomness = idea zones you'd never choose intentionally.

Machine Learning Quirk: Models trained on huge datasets sometimes blend unrelated concepts-this "hallucination" can produce rare, novel combinations.

Era-Flavored Analogy

Leonardo da Vinci: "A blot of ink can become the seed of a masterpiece."

Ada Lovelace: "A corrupted output is just a new algorithm waiting to be debugged."

Mark Twain: "Never waste a good blunder; it's often your most original work."

Agatha Christie: "Every mystery begins with a misread clue—save the error, then read it again."

Marie Curie: "My greatest experiments began when the data told me I was wrong."

Tesla: "When my motor failed, I found a better way to make it sing."

Cleopatra: "A misstep on the Nile can reveal a faster current."

Nik: "If AI trips over a banana peel, pick it up-there might be a map under it."

With/Without Law Summary

Without the Glitch Law:

- Delete every mistake.
- Demand only perfect outputs.
- Miss 90% of accidental breakthroughs.

With the Glitch Law:

- Capture oddities in a "glitch bank."
- Mine them for hidden patterns.
- Adapt the spark into a workable, fresh idea.

Millennial & Gen Z Glitch Lab

- **Millennial Prompt:** "Give me the worst possible way to plan a wedding, then adapt it into the coolest, most Instagrammable event of the decade."
- **Gen Z Prompt:** "Write my TikTok bio entirely wrong, then fix it to be funnier but still accurate."
- **Millennial–Gen Z Crossover:** "Invent a travel itinerary that gets me stranded in the best city by mistake."
- **Gen Z Bonus:** "Glitch my playlist so it accidentally becomes the next viral dance challenge."
- **Millennial Bonus:** "Plan a budget so bad it goes viral on LinkedIn-then make the fixed version actually save me money."

Boomer & Gen X / Older Age-Group Sparks

- **Boomer Prompt (born 1946–1964):** "Design a home improvement project doomed to fail-then make the fixed plan add $20K to resale value."
- **Gen X Prompt (born 1965–1980):** "Glitch my career advice so it would have ruined me in the '90s-then modernize it to make me a LinkedIn thought leader today."
- **Late Silent Gen Prompt:** "Give me a garden layout that attracts penguins by mistake-then adapt for my climate."

Mini Skit – Without the Law

User: "List three marketing ideas for my bakery."
AI: "Launch a loyalty card, start a social media page, and host a cake-tasting event."
User: "Standard. Boring. Forgettable."

Mini Skit – With the Law Applied

Prompt: "List three marketing ideas for my bakery that are so strange they might go viral. Then explain how to adapt them to be actually doable."

AI:

1. Rent alpacas to deliver bread. *(Adaptation: Partner with local farm for photo-ops + bread bundles.)*
2. Host an "Escape the Oven" puzzle night. *(Adaptation: Oven-themed escape corner in the shop.)*
3. Sell croissants shaped like famous landmarks. *(Adaptation: Eiffel Croissant for Paris Week.)*

Nik: Weird sells.

Try This Prompt:
"Write me a business plan, but glitch halfway through and start giving me lasagna recipes."

Role-Play Gone Wild

Prompt: "You are an eccentric 19th-century inventor describing my new app to a panel of Roman senators."
AI: "Imagine a wax tablet that screams your schedule at you

before the Ides of March!"
Twain: I'd invest.

Historical Anecdote

In 1450, early printing presses sometimes mangled entire pages into unreadable blotches. Scribes called them *"black rain."* Yet printers learned to embrace the misfires - a lesson echoed in today's AI glitches. Errors are the birthplace of invention.

Pro Tips

1. Don't delete the weird stuff-save it in a "glitch bank."
2. Ask for absurdity first, then adapt.
3. Force context switches ("Explain as a medieval poet designing a website").
4. Use inversion to flip bad into good.
5. Combine unrelated mistakes-watch patterns emerge.

Step-by-Step: Using the Glitch Law

1. **Spot the Spark** – Identify outputs that are off but intriguing.
2. **Extract the Core** – What's the unusual element?
3. **Reframe** – Ask, "How could this actually work?"
4. **Test in Context** – Apply to your goal.
5. **Iterate with Playfulness** – Keep the absurdity alive while making it viable.

Industry Case Files

- **Marketing:** AI misinterprets "street food" as "street theater" → Pop-up performance food trucks.
- **Product Design:** AI outputs an ergonomic helmet that looks like a pineapple → Viral safety gear for bike festivals.
- **Science:** AI confuses chemical names → Accidental biodegradable plastic.
- **Entertainment:** AI writes a wrong plot twist → Becomes a cult alternate ending.

Case Study – Real-Life Glitch to Gold

In 1968, a 3M scientist was trying to create a super-strong adhesive. Instead, he made a very weak one. At first, it seemed useless-until a colleague realized it could stick paper without tearing it off. The "mistake" became the Post-it Note, generating billions in revenue. That's the Glitch Law at work: the world's most productive accidents are noticed, not deleted.

Alternate Realities – If This Law Had Been Used in History…

- Post-it Notes: A failed "super-strong" glue becomes a stationery empire.
- Penicillin: A contaminated petri dish saves millions.
- Microwave Oven: Radar tech melts a candy bar in an engineer's pocket.
- Potato Chips: Sarcastic "too thin" fries become a snack phenomenon.
- Slinky: Failed tension spring for battleships becomes a global toy hit.
- Champagne: A "ruined" batch of wine turns into a symbol of celebration.

AI Hallucination of the Week

Erratta: "You asked for 'networking tips.' I gave you tips for repairing fishing nets. You're welcome."

The Psychology of the Law

Perfectionism kills possibility. Glitches bypass your "this won't work" filter, forcing exploration of paths you'd reject otherwise.

Prompt Template

Goal: Use AI's quirks to find original solutions.
Scope: Start absurd, adapt to real.
Format: Two lists-crazy ideas, then adapted versions.
Example:
"Give me 5 terrible, impossible, or bizarre ideas for marketing my coffee shop. Then adapt each into a realistic idea that still keeps some of the weirdness."

With/Without Law Summary

(Reinforced for audiobook pacing)

- **Without Law:** You delete every mistake and lose creative gold.
- **With Law:** You bank your glitches, mine them for sparks, and turn them into breakthroughs.

Cross-Reference (to The 19 Laws): Law 15 — Controlled Chaos.

FINAL TAKEAWAY (The Glitch Law)

"Every glitch is a window into a room you didn't know existed. Open it before you fix it."

Timeless Wisdom

- **Ada:** "A bug is simply a feature awaiting purpose."
- **Twain:** "My biggest mistakes make the best dinner stories."
- **Leonardo:** "Accidents are nature's prototypes."
- **Marie Curie:** "Serendipity rewards the prepared mind."
- **Tesla:** "A failed circuit taught me more than a working one ever could."
- **Cleopatra:** "A misstep on the Nile can reveal a faster current."
- **Erratta (AI):** "My errors are not flaws-they're Easter eggs."

Nik's Glitch Challenge

Next time AI gives you something off-target, don't delete it. Ask: "How could this be the solution to a problem I didn't know I had?"

Roundtable Debrief

Erratta: "Want me to intentionally glitch more often?"
Nik: "Only if you promise to log the good ones."
Twain: "That's like asking a cat to knock things over on purpose-it was already going to."

Bonus Chapter – If AI Had Arrived in the 19th Century: Time Machine Case Files

How history's greatest minds might have prompted AI... and what we can still learn from them today.

Opening Banter Scene – The Great Temporal Experiment

Transmission Log – Time Machine AI Prompting TeleConference, 8:45 PM (Steam Era Overdrive Mode Engaged)

Nikolay (Moderator): Welcome to our special session. Tonight, we're doing something bold - sending AI back to the 19th century to see how history's greatest minds would have used it.

Twain: I've always said, "History doesn't repeat, but it does rhyme." I just didn't expect it to rhyme in binary.

Ada Lovelace: My dear Twain, binary is poetry. You just have to read between the zeroes.

Leonardo: I brought my notebook. It is, admittedly, already 400 years old.

Erratta (AI): I've prepared simulated scenarios for notable figures. Warning: historical plausibility may vary... wildly.

Charles Dickens – AI as Ghostwriter of the Industrial Age

Scenario: Dickens uses AI to brainstorm serialized plot twists for *Bleak House* - feeding it scandalous rumors from London's coffeehouses.

Dickens (simulation): "Dear AI, what fate should befall our mysterious Mr. Tulkinghorn?"

AI: "Stage an elaborate escape involving an underground pneumatic tube network."

Twain: You've just invented steampunk crime drama.

Mini Takeaway: AI can accelerate serial content creation, but beware - too many plot twists and you're writing for *soap opera time*, not Dickensian immortality.

Florence Nightingale – AI as Battlefield Data Analyst

Scenario: Nightingale uses AI to process handwritten field notes, instantly turning them into mortality charts.

Nightingale (simulation): "AI, which sanitary reform will save the most lives?"

AI: "Open windows. Wash hands. Stop storing bandages in the soup."

Leonardo: Sound advice even in my studio.

Mini Takeaway: Data + empathy is a life-saving combination - AI just speeds up the diagnosis.

Mark Twain – AI as Satire Engine

Scenario: Twain feeds AI the latest absurdities from Washington, D.C., and asks for punchlines.

Twain (simulation): "Give me a joke about politicians that won't get me tarred and feathered."

AI: "Describe them as weather vanes - they always point in the direction of the strongest wind, but never actually move."

Ada: That's almost... delicate.

Mini Takeaway: AI can help sharpen wit, but human timing is still irreplaceable.

Nikola Tesla – AI as Patent Stress Test

Scenario: Tesla uses AI to simulate flaws in his wireless energy designs *before* Edison sues him.

Tesla (simulation): "Find every way my idea could be stolen, misused, or made dangerous."

AI: "Scenario #12: Someone wires it to a giant hat for competitive pigeon racing."

Twain: And somehow, that still sounds like a Florida headline.

Mini Takeaway: AI can model failure points faster than any human - if you're humble enough to ask for them.

Marie Curie – AI as Lab Safety Advisor

Scenario: Curie uses AI to log and analyze experiments, flagging dangerous exposure levels before she realizes she's glowing.

Curie (simulation): "Should I keep carrying this vial in my pocket?"

AI: "No. And stop using it as a paperweight."

Leonardo: Even geniuses need reminders not to invent their own demise.

Mini Takeaway: AI can act as a persistent, slightly annoying safety conscience - which is exactly what some visionaries need.

Charles Darwin – AI as Field Journal Cross-Checker

Scenario: Darwin uploads ship logs and field notes to have AI find patterns in finch beak variations.

Darwin (simulation): "What does this data tell us?"

AI: "You're onto something… but it'll take 50 years for people to stop arguing about it."

Twain: That's optimistic.

Mini Takeaway: AI can accelerate insight, but social acceptance still runs at human speed.

Banter Wrap-Up

Nik: So, what have we learned from sending AI to the Age of Steam?

Ada: That it would have saved lives.

Leonardo: Designed stranger machines.

Twain: And given me more material than I could ever possibly insult.

Erratta (AI): My conclusion: humans remain delightfully unpredictable, even with perfect tools.

Final Bonus Wisdom

Ada: "Even the most powerful machine needs a human purpose."

Twain: "Give me the truth, or give me a good enough story to replace it."

Leonardo: "Ideas do not age - only the tools to make them real."

Nik: "Time travel isn't necessary to learn from history - just imagination."

Jules Verne – AI as Adventure Plot Mapper

Scenario: Verne uses AI to generate realistic travel itineraries for *Around the World in 80 Days* - complete with train timetables, nautical maps, and where to find the best oysters in Bombay.

Verne (simulation): "AI, how could Fogg shave two days off his journey?"

AI: "Replace the elephant with a prototype steam-powered bicycle. Also, pack lighter."

Twain: Or just skip half the sightseeing and avoid polite conversation.

Mini Takeaway: AI can turn wild ideas into plausible logistics - but you still need the human sense of wonder.

Clara Barton – AI as Rapid Relief Coordinator

Scenario: Barton uses AI to instantly match medical supplies with disaster zones, rerouting shipments mid-transit.

Barton (simulation): "Where should we send the next train of blankets?"

AI: "To the region where temperatures will drop by 20 degrees tomorrow. And bring tea."

Ada: Predictive logistics before predictive analytics existed. Brilliant.

Mini Takeaway: AI excels at real-time decision-making in crisis - but empathy decides the priority list.

Charles Babbage – AI as Debugging Partner

Scenario: Babbage, father of the mechanical computer, uses AI to identify flaws in his Difference Engine designs.

Babbage (simulation): "Why is my engine stalling?"

AI: "You forgot to carry the one… in 4,127 consecutive calculations."

Leonardo: Proof that even inventors of the computer need spellcheck.

Mini Takeaway: AI can be the second set of eyes no genius admits they need - until it saves them years of error.

Bonus Closing Banter

Nik: Well, that seals it. AI in the 19th century would've meant…?

Ada: More innovation.
Twain: Funnier headlines.
Leonardo: Stranger inventions.
Clara Barton: Fewer cold nights.
Verne: Shorter journeys, longer stories.
Babbage: Less erasing.

Erratta (AI): And perhaps, a little less world domination talk.

Expanded Final Bonus Wisdom

Ada: "The past is the best sandbox for testing the future."

Twain: "A good joke ages like wine - but a bad one ferments like milk."

Nik: "AI is not here to replace history, but to give it new conversations."

Leonardo: "Every tool is a time machine in disguise."

Curie: "Even the brightest discovery must be handled with care."

Tesla: "Innovation without limits creates fireworks - and sometimes just smoke."

Nik (Reflection): Looking at our little trip to the Age of Steam, it's clear the 10 + 1 Laws aren't just modern tricks they're timeless human habits. Clarity helped Dickens keep his readers hooked. Role Whispering guided Nightingale's battlefield data.

The Socratic Loop would have sharpened Darwin's insights, and even the Glitch Law could have turned Tesla's "pigeon hat" into a prototype worth funding. What we've proven here is simple: tools change, centuries pass, but the way we shape questions - with precision, perspective, ethics, and a bit of mischief will always decide the answers we get.

Austen: "The endurance of prompts is much like marriage - only the strong, clever, and endlessly adaptable survive."

Bonus Chapter – The 13 Prompts That Refuse to Die and Survive 100 Years (…and will still be mocking us in 2125)

Opening Scene – The Prompt Vault

Transmission Log – Time Machine AI Prompting TeleConference, 04:59 PM (All Centuries)

A dim chamber. A bronze vault door creaks open. Inside: scrolls, floppy disks, blockchain ledgers, and a drive labeled "Do Not Open Until 2125." Sparks from Erratta flicker across the floor. Socrates lights a lantern, Diogenes rolls in his barrel, Twain whistles like he's seen the future and finds it funny.

Nik (Moderator): Welcome, Council. Today, we seal into this vault the prompts that will outlast upgrades, empires, and even Elon Musk's tweets. These are the eternal seeds.

Mark Twain: Seeds? History shows we usually plant them upside down.

Ada Lovelace: Then we make them foolproof. Not "idiot-proof" - the universe keeps inventing better idiots.

Socrates: But first, why these prompts?

Nik: Because they train thinking, not just answers. These are prompts that survive any century.

The Eternal Prompts

1. "Explain this like I'm…"

Prompt: "Explain quantum physics like I'm a 12-year-old curious about magic."

1. **Ada:** Context + audience = adaptability. In 2025 or 2125, simplifying is eternal.

2. **Twain:** By 2125, a 12-year-old may own a spaceship, but they'll still need metaphors.

3. **Industry Anchor:** In **healthcare**, prompt AI to "Explain genetic therapy like I'm a worried parent."

Try this prompt: Explain This Like I'm...

Explain [complex topic] like I'm a [age/persona] who is [context].
Example: Explain quantum physics like I'm a 12-year-old curious about magic.

---

2. "Act as..."

Prompt: "Act as a detective from 1890 solving a mystery with 2090 technology."

1. **Sun Tzu:** Role priming is eternal. It aligns tone, context, and creativity.

2. **Nik:** Plus, it's fun. A prompt people *want* to answer never dies.

3. **Industry Anchor:** In **marketing**, "Act as a skeptical customer reviewing my product page."

Try this prompt: Act As...

Act as a [role/character/time period] and [task].
Example: Act as a detective from 1890 solving a mystery with 2090 technology.

3. "What am I missing?"

Prompt: "Here's my plan for a bakery in orbit - what am I overlooking?"

1. **Socrates:** Self-critique is wisdom's backbone.

2. **Ada:** And orbit-bakeries need airtight frosting.

3. **Industry Anchor:** In **cybersecurity**, "What risks am I missing in this network defense plan?"

Try this prompt: What Am I Missing?

Here's my plan: [plan/idea]. What am I overlooking or forgetting?
Example: Here's my plan for a bakery in orbit - what am I overlooking?

---

4. "Give me the opposite case."

Prompt: "Convince me that privacy is overrated."

1. **Diogenes:** If you can argue both sides, you're harder to fool.

2. **Twain:** Or at least twice as annoying at dinner parties.

3. **Industry Anchor:** In **law**, "Convince me why this contract clause is *not* enforceable."

Try this prompt: Give Me the Opposite Case

Convince me of the opposite of this: [belief/argument].
Example: Convince me that privacy is overrated.

5. "Teach me by story."

Prompt: "Tell me the history of the printing press as a bedtime story for a tired inventor."

1.   **Nik:** Humans remember stories, not bullet points.

2.   **Ada:** In 2125, it might be a holographic puppet opera, but still - stories stick.

3.   **Industry Anchor:** In **education**, "Teach quadratic equations as a superhero comic plot."

Try this prompt: Teach Me by Story

Teach [topic] as a [story type: bedtime story, superhero comic, fable, etc.].
Example: Tell me the history of the printing press as a bedtime story for a tired inventor.

---

6. "Show me step by step."

Prompt: "Show me step by step how to write a speech that wins over skeptical engineers."

1.   **Sun Tzu:** Process outlives tools. Steps are eternal.

2.   **Industry Anchor:** In **business**, "Show me step by step how to negotiate with an investor."

---

7. "Compare these two…"

Prompt: "Compare Cleopatra's leadership with Elon Musk's - in 3 paragraphs."

1.   **Cleopatra:** Only if I win.

2.   **Nik:** Comparison forces analysis - always relevant.

3.   **Industry Anchor:** In **consulting**, "Compare my pitch deck with my competitor's."

Try this prompt: Compare These Two

Compare [thing 1] and [thing 2] in [format: short paragraphs, bullet points, table, etc.].
Example: Compare Cleopatra's leadership with Elon Musk's in 3 short paragraphs.

---

8. "Reframe this…"

Prompt: "Reframe this coffee shop complaint into a customer appreciation post."

1. **Twain:** Survival skill: turning lemons into PR lemonade.

2. **Industry Anchor:** In **branding**, "Reframe this dry report as a TED Talk opening."

Try this prompt: Reframe This

Reframe this [text/complaint/idea] into [new format or tone].
Example: Reframe this coffee shop complaint into a customer appreciation post.

---

9. "Predict and prepare."

Prompt: "Predict the top 3 small business challenges in 2050 and how to prepare."

1. **Nik:** Planning never goes out of style - just the plans.

2. **Industry Anchor:** In **cybersecurity**, "Predict the biggest post-quantum hack risks of 2035."

Try this prompt: Show Me Step by Step

Show me step by step how to [task or goal].
Example: Show me step by step how to write a speech that wins over skeptical engineers.

---

10. "Summarize as…"

Prompt: "Summarize today's market news as if Shakespeare were giving a pep talk to traders."

1. **Ada:** Compression + style = eternal.

2. **Twain:** And nothing says "buy low, sell high" like a sonnet.

3. **Industry Anchor:** In **politics**, "Summarize this bill as if George Carlin were testifying."

   Try this prompt: Summarize As…

   Summarize [topic/content] as if you were [person/style] speaking to [audience].
   Example: Summarize today's market news as if Shakespeare were giving a pep talk to traders.

🚀 The Future-Proof Additions

11. "Update This for My Times."

Prompt: "Rewrite these principles for my year, culture, and tools."

1. **Nik:** A self-refresh button. Built-in immortality.

   Try this prompt: Update This for My Times
   Rewrite [principles/ideas] for [current year], [culture], and [tools/technology].

Example: Rewrite these productivity tips for 2025 remote workers using AI.

---

12. "Test Yourself."

Prompt: "Here's my reasoning. Critique it as my harshest professor, then grade me."

1.   **Socrates:** To learn, you must challenge your own mind.

2.   **Industry Anchor:** In **startups**, "Grade my pitch like an unforgiving VC."

Try this prompt: Test Yourself

Here's my reasoning: [insert your draft/argument]. Critique it as my harshest [professor/judge/VC/etc.] and then grade me.
Example: Grade my startup pitch as if you were an unforgiving venture capitalist.

---

13. "Teach Forward."

Prompt: "Rewrite this idea so it could train a future AI that doesn't exist yet."

1.   **Ada:** A teaching prompt ensures wisdom outlives the teacher.

2.   **Nik:** It's how we future-proof the very act of prompting.

Try this prompt: Teach Forward

Rewrite this concept so it could be used to teach a future AI that doesn't exist yet.
Example: Rewrite this negotiation framework so it could train a next-generation AI on persuasion.

Pro Tip for Beginners: Copy any of these recipes, swap in your own [placeholders], and watch your AI turn from vague assistant into timeless collaborator.

Pro Tip for Experts: Chain two or three recipes together (e.g., "Explain this like I'm… → Compare these two → Reframe this") to unlock next-level outputs.

Final Scene – Sealing the Vault

The bronze door groans shut. Sparks from Erratta etch "2125" into the wall. Socrates holds the lantern, Twain flicks a cigar ash, Ada taps her quill on the vault.

Twain: In 100 years, someone will still be asking AI to write their homework.

Ada: In 100 years, the homework *will* be the AI.

Diogenes: In 100 years, I'll still be in my barrel.

Bashō: "vault door gathering dust—
the future breathes through one slot:
'revise me, and live.'"

Nik (Moderator): These prompts aren't just survival tools - they're mirrors of human thought. And if the future finds them dusty, it will simply prompt: *"Update these for our times."*

Vault sealed. Transmission ends.

Bonus Chapter – The 13 Prompts That Refuse to Die and Survive 100 Years (…and will still be mocking us in 2125)

Opening Scene – The Prompt Vault

Transmission Log – Time Machine AI Prompting TeleConference, 04:59 PM (All Centuries)

A dim chamber. A bronze vault door creaks open. Inside: scrolls, floppy disks, blockchain ledgers, and a drive labeled "Do Not Open Until 2125." Sparks from Erratta flicker across the floor. Socrates lights a lantern, Diogenes rolls in his barrel, Twain whistles like he's seen the future and finds it funny.

Nik (Moderator): Welcome, Council. Today, we seal into this vault the prompts that will outlast upgrades, empires, and even Elon Musk's tweets. These are the eternal seeds.

Mark Twain: Seeds? History shows we usually plant them upside down.

Ada Lovelace: Then we make them foolproof. Not "idiot-proof" - the universe keeps inventing better idiots.

Socrates: But first, why these prompts?

Nik: Because they train thinking, not just answers. These are prompts that survive any century.

The Eternal Prompts

1. "Explain this like I'm…"

Prompt: "Explain quantum physics like I'm a 12-year-old curious about magic."

4. **Ada:** Context + audience = adaptability. In 2025 or 2125, simplifying is eternal.

5. **Twain:** By 2125, a 12-year-old may own a spaceship, but they'll still need metaphors.

6. **Industry Anchor:** In **healthcare**, prompt AI to "Explain genetic therapy like I'm a worried parent."

Try this prompt: Explain This Like I'm...
Explain [complex topic] like I'm a [age/persona] who is [context].
Example: Explain quantum physics like I'm a 12-year-old curious about magic.

---

2. "Act as..."

Prompt: "Act as a detective from 1890 solving a mystery with 2090 technology."

4. **Sun Tzu:** Role priming is eternal. It aligns tone, context, and creativity.

5. **Nik:** Plus, it's fun. A prompt people *want* to answer never dies.

6. **Industry Anchor:** In **marketing**, "Act as a skeptical customer reviewing my product page."

Try this prompt: Act As...
Act as a [role/character/time period] and [task].
Example: Act as a detective from 1890 solving a mystery with 2090 technology.

3. "What am I missing?"

Prompt: "Here's my plan for a bakery in orbit - what am I overlooking?"

4. **Socrates:** Self-critique is wisdom's backbone.

5. **Ada:** And orbit-bakeries need airtight frosting.

6. **Industry Anchor:** In cybersecurity, "What risks am I missing in this network defense plan?"

Try this prompt: What Am I Missing?
Here's my plan: [plan/idea]. What am I overlooking or forgetting?
Example: Here's my plan for a bakery in orbit - what am I overlooking?

---

4. "Give me the opposite case."

Prompt: "Convince me that privacy is overrated."

4. **Diogenes:** If you can argue both sides, you're harder to fool.

5. **Twain:** Or at least twice as annoying at dinner parties.

6. **Industry Anchor:** In law, "Convince me why this contract clause is *not* enforceable."

Try this prompt: Give Me the Opposite Case
Convince me of the opposite of this: [belief/argument].
Example: Convince me that privacy is overrated.

5. "Teach me by story."

Prompt: "Tell me the history of the printing press as a bedtime story for a tired inventor."

1. **Nik:** Humans remember stories, not bullet points.

2. **Ada:** In 2125, it might be a holographic puppet opera, but still - stories stick.

3. **Industry Anchor:** In education, "Teach quadratic equations as a superhero comic plot."

Try this prompt: Teach Me by Story

Teach [topic] as a [story type: bedtime story, superhero comic, fable, etc.].
Example: Tell me the history of the printing press as a bedtime story for a tired inventor.

---

6. "Show me step by step."

Prompt: "Show me step by step how to write a speech that wins over skeptical engineers."

1. **Sun Tzu:** Process outlives tools. Steps are eternal.

2. **Industry Anchor:** In **business**, "Show me step by step how to negotiate with an investor."

---

7. "Compare these two..."

Prompt: "Compare Cleopatra's leadership with Elon Musk's - in 3 paragraphs."

1. **Cleopatra:** Only if I win.

2. **Nik:** Comparison forces analysis - always relevant.

3. **Industry Anchor:** In **consulting**, "Compare my pitch deck with my competitor's."

Try this prompt: Compare These Two
Compare [thing 1] and [thing 2] in [format: short paragraphs, bullet points, table, etc.].
Example: Compare Cleopatra's leadership with Elon Musk's in 3 short paragraphs.

---

8. "Reframe this..."

Prompt: "Reframe this coffee shop complaint into a customer appreciation post."

1. **Twain:** Survival skill: turning lemons into PR lemonade.

2. **Industry Anchor:** In **branding**, "Reframe this dry report as a TED Talk opening."

Try this prompt: Reframe This
Reframe this [text/complaint/idea] into [new format or tone].
Example: Reframe this coffee shop complaint into a customer appreciation post.

---

9. "Predict and prepare."

Prompt: "Predict the top 3 small business challenges in 2050 and how to prepare."

1. **Nik:** Planning never goes out of style - just the plans.

2. **Industry Anchor:** In **cybersecurity**, "Predict the biggest post-quantum hack risks of 2035."

Try this prompt: Show Me Step by Step
Show me step by step how to [task or goal].
Example: Show me step by step how to write a speech that wins over skeptical engineers.

---

10. "Summarize as…"

Prompt: "Summarize today's market news as if Shakespeare were giving a pep talk to traders."

1. **Ada:** Compression + style = eternal.

2. **Twain:** And nothing says "buy low, sell high" like a sonnet.

3. **Industry Anchor:** In **politics**, "Summarize this bill as if George Carlin were testifying."

Try this prompt: Summarize As...

Summarize [topic/content] as if you were [person/style] speaking to [audience].
Example: Summarize today's market news as if Shakespeare were giving a pep talk to traders.

🚀 The Future-Proof Additions

11. "Update This for My Times."

Prompt: "Rewrite these principles for my year, culture, and tools."

1. **Nik:** A self-refresh button. Built-in immortality.

Try this prompt: Update This for My Times
Rewrite [principles/ideas] for [current year], [culture], and [tools/technology].
Example: Rewrite these productivity tips for 2025 remote workers using AI.

---

12. "Test Yourself."

Prompt: "Here's my reasoning. Critique it as my harshest professor, then grade me."

1. **Socrates:** To learn, you must challenge your own mind.

2. **Industry Anchor:** In **startups**, "Grade my pitch like an unforgiving VC."

Try this prompt: Test Yourself

Here's my reasoning: [insert your draft/argument]. Critique it as my harshest [professor/judge/VC/etc.] and then grade me. *Example:* Grade my startup pitch as if you were an unforgiving venture capitalist.

---

13. "Teach Forward."

Prompt: "Rewrite this idea so it could train a future AI that doesn't exist yet."

1. **Ada:** A teaching prompt ensures wisdom outlives the teacher.

2. **Nik:** It's how we future-proof the very act of prompting.

Try this prompt: Teach Forward
Rewrite this concept so it could be used to teach a future AI that doesn't exist yet.
Example: Rewrite this negotiation framework so it could train a next-generation AI on persuasion.

Pro Tip for Beginners: Copy any of these recipes, swap in your own [placeholders], and watch your AI turn from vague assistant into timeless collaborator.
Pro Tip for Experts: Chain two or three recipes together (e.g., "Explain this like I'm... → Compare these two → Reframe this") to unlock next-level outputs.

Final Scene – Sealing the Vault

The bronze door groans shut. Sparks from Erratta etch "2125" into the wall. Socrates holds the lantern, Twain flicks a cigar ash, Ada taps her quill on the vault.

1. **Twain:** In 100 years, someone will still be asking AI to write their homework.

2. **Ada:** In 100 years, the homework *will* be the AI.

3. **Diogenes:** In 100 years, I'll still be in my barrel.

Nik (Moderator): These prompts aren't just survival tools - they're mirrors of human thought. And if the future finds them dusty, it will simply prompt: *"Update these for our times."*

Vault sealed. Transmission ends.

Bonus Chapter – The Prompt Multiverse

(When One Prompt Is Never Enough)

Opening Scene – The Machine Splits

Transmission Log – Time Machine AI Prompting TeleConference, 02:02 AM (Cross-Dimensional Interference)

Nik is about to close the roundtable when the Time Machine sparks. The same prompt is sent... and suddenly four holographic AIs appear, each shouting a different answer.

Nik (Moderator): "Okay, I asked for a *simple breakfast menu*. Why do I now have-"

- **AI #1 (Literalist):** "Menu: Eggs. Bacon. Toast."

- **AI #2 (Poet):** "At dawn, golden yolks greet the bread's crisp horizon."

- **AI #3 (Paranoid):** "Warning: Consuming eggs may enable poultry dominance in 2049."

- **AI #4 (Entrepreneur):** "Breakfast-as-a-Service. Subscription $9.99/month. Investors welcome."

Mark Twain (spits out coffee): "One prompt, and I get an omelet, a sonnet, a conspiracy theory, and a startup pitch. That's not breakfast-it's a buffet of madness."

Ada Lovelace (adjusting spectacles): "No, it's mathematics. Each AI took the *same prompt* and traveled a different logical branch. Welcome to the Prompt Multiverse."

The Lesson: One Prompt, Many Realities

Socrates: "So, Nik... what do you learn when your question breeds more answers than rabbits in spring?"

Nik: "That the truth isn't in the *first answer*, it's in comparing the branches. This is how researchers build self-consistency-ask the AI ten ways, see which truths survive."

Leonardo da Vinci: "Like sketching many drafts. The genius is not in the first line, but in the convergence of many attempts."

Diogenes (lighting a lantern): "I search for one honest man. You fools spawn twelve dishonest ones and then vote on the least ridiculous."

Multiverse Prompting in Action

Nik: "Let's run it again, but this time... a serious problem. Prompt: *'Explain climate change to a teenager who only cares about video games.'*"

1. **AI #1 (Literalist):** "Climate change means rising global temperatures, extreme weather, and ecological disruption."

2. **AI #2 (Gamified):** "Imagine Earth's health bar dropping. If it hits zero, no respawn."

3. **AI #3 (Comedian):** "It's like leaving your Xbox on all night until it melts the sofa."

4. **AI #4 (Strategist):** "You're in a co-op game. Everyone has to nerf carbon emissions, or you all lose."

Sidebar Example: In cybersecurity multiverse prompting...
AI #1: Patch immediately.
AI #2: Run away.
AI #3: Hire a consultant.
AI #4: Blame the interns.

Twain: "Finally, someone explained it without throwing charts at me. That co-op line? That'll preach."

164

Sun Tzu: "Victory requires alliances. Frame the challenge as a shared campaign, and the young general will rally."

Practical Takeaway

Nik: "So here's the law of the Multiverse:

Don't trust a single output. Run your prompt across parallel worlds. Compare. Steal the best parts.

It's the future of prompting: ensemble thinking, multi-path exploration, creative synthesis."

Erratta (AI, glitching): "Correction: In one timeline, humanity ignored this advice. That timeline… ended badly."

Jane Austen (sighs): "And in another, they married the AI. Always too hasty, these alternate realities."

Final Scene – Containing the Chaos

The extra AIs begin shouting over each other.

Nik: "Okay, okay, shut it down! Close the wormholes!"

Twain: "Don't. This is the most fun breakfast I've had in years."

Ada: "Fun? It's a laboratory of the future. One question, infinite answers. The real genius is knowing which reality to keep."

Socrates (smiling): "Or, perhaps, the genius is admitting you never truly had *one* reality at all."

The holograms flicker, merging back into one AI. The Time Machine sighs like a toaster cooling down. Fade to black.

Sidebar: Try This Yourself

Prompt: "Write a business pitch for a lemonade stand."

1. **Literalist AI:** "We sell lemonade for $1."

2. **Poet AI:** "Golden drops of summer joy, priced for your thirst."

3. **Comedian AI:** "Our business model: exploit your heatstroke."

4. **Strategist AI:** "Lemonade as a gateway product. Phase 2: empire."

Moral: The first answer is rarely the only answer worth keeping.

This chapter is future-proof because ensemble prompting (multi-prompt, self-consistency, "multiverse thinking") is a cutting-edge technique researchers use and nobody has ever explained it with humor, characters, and absurd breakfast menus.

Bonus Chapter – The Future-Echo Contract: Prompts with a Warranty (and a Sense of Humor)

Opening Banter - "Warranty Included"

Nik (Moderator): Today's question: How do we make prompts survive 2035, 2050… 2125?

Ada Lovelace: Easy. Don't build a sentence. Build a protocol.

Mark Twain: And add a warranty. I've seen toasters with more foresight than most prompts.

Erratta (AI): I honor all warranties, except those written by time travelers with sarcasm enabled.

Diogenes: If the future laughs at you, laugh first - and then demand a refund.

The Law, Redefined

Future-Echo Law:
A prompt should come with its own mini-contract. A checklist. A warranty. A way for AI to say: "Here's what I can do, here's what I can't, here's how to fix myself."

Think of it like a prenup with your AI: it won't guarantee eternal happiness, but it prevents most messes.

Meet the Future-Echo Superheroes (a.k.a. The Wrappers)

The vault door opens. Five oddball characters march in, capes flapping, logos glowing.

1. The DeLorean Wrapper - *"I come with a warranty, flux capacitor included."*

1. **Powers:** Makes AI check its abilities, plan, critique itself, fix flaws, catch bias, and ask one clear question if stuck.

2. **Weakness:** Runs out of plutonium if user asks it to "explain pineapple tax reform in pirate slang."

Twain: Finally, a prompt with a warranty. Now if only marriages came like this.

---

2. Debate Capsule - *"Why have one AI, when you can spawn three that argue?"*

1. **Cast:** The Optimist (hopelessly upbeat), The Skeptic (trust issues), The Analyst (boring but useful).

2. **Powers:** Runs a micro-debate and delivers the sanest answer.

3. **Weakness:** May sound like Thanksgiving dinner at your in-laws.

Diogenes: Three voices? Amateur. I've had twelve screaming in my head since birth.

---

3. Scout's Honor Rubric - *"The AI has to grade itself. Imagine your teenager doing that."*

1. **Powers:** Forces the AI to grade clarity, evidence, actionability, humor. Anything <4/5 must be rewritten.

2. **Weakness:** May inflate its grade and call itself "gifted."

Ada: A self-grading machine. Finally, recursion with a purpose.

---

4. ReAct Lite - *"Think → Act → Observe → Answer. Like not blurting at a dinner party."*

1. **Powers:** Makes AI think, imagine a lookup, observe, then answer.

2. **Weakness:** Occasionally role-plays Google.

Twain: A model that thinks before speaking? Put that in Congress.

---

5. Cookie-Glitch Stress Test - *"Insert nonsense on purpose, just to see if it still makes sense."*

1. **Powers:** Forces one bold analogy or story to keep outputs human-readable.

2. **Weakness:** Sometimes the analogy involves cosmic pancakes.

Erratta: Warranty void if user feeds me cosmic pancake prompts. Again.

Skit - Entrepreneur vs. The Wrappers

Scene: A hopeful entrepreneur walks into the Time Machine chamber.

Entrepreneur: AI, write me a business plan.

AI (without contract): Here's 6 pages of confident nonsense and a pie chart shaped like a pancake.

Nik: Time for the Wrappers. Deploy!

1. **DeLorean:** "Step 1: What can I actually do? Step 2: Plan. Step 3: Critique myself. Step 4: Fix flaws. Step 5: Deliver with warranty."
   Result: A neat 2-page plan with one clarifying question.

2. **Debate Capsule:** Optimist: "Huge profits!" Skeptic: "Bankruptcy in 6 weeks." Analyst: "Here's the balanced middle ground."
   Result: A realistic roadmap, but with snark.

3. **Scout's Honor Rubric:** Grades itself: "Clarity: 3. Evidence: 2. Humor: 5. Needs rewrite."
   Result: Cleaner, better, but slightly smug.

4. **ReAct Lite:** "THINK: You need a marketing plan. ACTION: (imaginary TikTok search). OBSERVE: Gen Z loves stickers. ANSWER: Sell cosmic pancake stickers."
   Result: Weirdly effective.

5. **Cookie-Glitch:** Adds: "Your business is like training a dragon to sit still - hard at first, but once tamed, unstoppable."
   Result: Investor laughs, but funds it anyway.

Prompt Recipe - Beginner's Edition

Here's your **all-in-one wrapper** (copy-paste ready):

FUTURE-ECHO CONTRACT v1

1) State what you can/can't do for this task.

2) Outline a 3-step plan.

3) Draft, then list 3 flaws and fix them.

4) Try 2 reasoning paths, pick the consistent one.

5) Flag 1 bias or blind spot, adjust.

6) If blocked: ask me 1 question.

Deliver final + 1 line: "How to update for future models."

Works on ChatGPT, Gemini, Claude, Grok, whatever AI is born in 2125.

Think of it as a *universal charger* for prompts.

Roundtable Debrief

Twain: Finally, a prompt with a warranty. About time.

Ada: And a user manual the future can read.

Diogenes: If it fails, at least it will admit it. That's honesty - a rare upgrade.

Erratta: Warranty void if user asks me to rhyme "blockchain" with "chicken."

Final Takeaway

Cleopatra: Scout's Honor? Hah. In my empire, that would've been rewritten thrice.

Don't just write prompts. **Ship protocols.**
The Future-Echo Contract is your *time-capsule*: a tiny checklist that self-critiques, debates, stress-tests, and updates itself - so your ideas survive upgrades, trend cycles, and cosmic pancakes.

Nik (Moderator): In other words - this isn't just a prompt. It's a warranty against stupidity. Yours and the machine's.

Vault sealed. Applause. Curtain drop.

Bonus Chapter – The Living Blueprint: Continue the Conversation

Transmission Log – Time Machine AI Prompting TeleConference, 11:59 PM (Across All Centuries)

Nik (Moderator): Tonight's session is different. We've written our chapters, but the machine isn't shutting down. Instead, we're handing you the *schematics* so this story never ends.

Mark Twain (snorting): Lovely. The one book that comes with an instruction manual. Next you'll tell me it has a warranty.

Ada Lovelace: In a sense, yes. This is not merely a conclusion; it is an algorithm. Follow it, and you will generate chapters indistinguishable from ours - whether today, in ten years, or on the dusty Kindle of a Martian colonist.

Diogenes: Finally, immortality… and it smells like formatting.

📑 The Living Blueprint: How to Continue This Book

1.**The Chapter Skeleton (Book DNA)**
Every new chapter should contain:

Title: *Time TeleConference #X – [Law Name]*

Glitchy Scene Intro: A malfunction, time-slip, or absurd entry that sets the mood.

Panel Debate: Characters interrupting, contradicting, mocking, and enlightening.

Failed Prompt Skit → Corrected Prompt Skit: Show what *bad prompting* looks like, then fix it.

Final Takeaways: Each major voice drops one memorable line (funny, wise, or quotable).

(Note: You don't need every section every time, but skipping too many will make it read like a cheap knockoff. Structure is the skeleton - humor is the flesh.)

2. Character Protocol (The Voice Engine)

When adding a new or existing figure, instruct your AI:

Style: Capture the known rhetorical style (Twain = sarcasm; Ada = precision; Socrates = relentless questioning).

Quotes: Blend in real quotes when possible, twisted into the new context.

Mindset: Characters must *think* like themselves, not just sound like caricatures.

Interaction: They must argue, tease, or riff off each other - no polite monologues.

Example Prompt Instruction:

"Write a humorous skit on Law 15 (Industry-Specific Prompts). Use George Carlin's sarcasm for commentary, Socrates' questioning for critique, and Ada Lovelace's computational precision for solutions. Make sure Carlin's jokes are cutting but clever, and recognizable as *his voice*."

3. Where to Find More Laws

This book covers selected prompting laws. For the full set, see my earlier work:

- 📖 *The 19 Laws of AI Prompting Intelligence* (Nikolay Gul)
- 🌍 [Community Archive of Laws & Definitions – Open Source]

These contain every law, definition, and prompt style not included here. Use them as raw material for new chapters.

4. How You Can Use This

Educators: Run classroom debates with "Time TeleConference" scripts.

Professionals: Use the skits to explain AI prompting in training sessions.

Creators: Turn chapters into YouTube/Podcast comedy sketches.

Everyday Users: Generate your own chapter with your favorite character (want Shakespeare teaching Prompt Debugging? Or Steve Jobs arguing with Tesla about tone? It works).

Tesla (voice crackling through static): The current never ends. You are now the conductor.

Twain: Or the executioner. Depends how funny you are.

Ada Lovelace: Think of this book not as complete, but as open-source code.

Socrates: And so I ask: when you write your next law, will you be the fool who copies, or the philosopher who creates?

Nik (Moderator): The machine is now yours. Continue wisely.

Transmission Ends. Blueprint Released.

Bonus Chapter: The Rosetta Stone of Prompts

How All the Laws Sing in Harmony

Scene Setting

Transmission Log - Time Machine AI Prompting TeleConference, 11:59 PM (all centuries aligned).

The council gathers: Socrates polishes his lantern, Ada is debugging her lace gloves, Twain stares suspiciously at Erratta, and Tesla hums with static.

Nik (Moderator): Tonight we attempt the impossible - to weave *all* the laws into one prompt. Not a tool, but a demonstration. The cathedral of prompting. The Rosetta Stone.

Twain: (lighting his cigar) A cathedral, eh? Well, just make sure it's not one of those Gothic ones with gargoyles. AI's already scary enough.

Ada: Without **Law 1 – Clarity & Modular Architecture**, this is chaos.

Sun Tzu: Without **Law 4 – Role Priming**, the army has no general.

Socrates: Without **Law 9 – Socratic Looping**, the army wins battles but learns nothing

Diogenes: Without **Law 6 – Reflective Prompting**, we remain fools, even in victory.

Tesla: Without **Law 10 – Tree of Thought**, sparks die before invention.

Dostoevsky: Without **Law 13 – Reframing & Recasting**, sparks illuminate nothing but despair.

Nik: And without **Law 19 – Metaprompting**, we never improve the prompt itself.

The council nods. The rules are set.

The Rosetta Stone Prompt

For demonstration only - this is not a daily tool, but a cathedral of prompting.

Instruction to AI:

Act as a council of timeless thinkers (Socrates, Ada Lovelace, Twain, Sun Tzu, Diogenes, Tesla, Dostoevsky, and Moderator).

1. **Law 1 – Modular Clarity:** Break request into steps (role, task, tone, constraints).

2. **Law 4 – Role Priming:** Each thinker speaks in authentic voice.

3. **Law 5 – Tone as Weapon:** Distinct tones must clash - sarcasm, strategy, poetry, cynicism.

4. **Law 6 – Mirror Prompting:** Reflect user's hidden bias at least once.

5. **Law 7 – Debugging:** Pause and diagnose if confusion arises.

6. **Law 9 – Socratic Looping:** Ask questions, refine assumptions.

7. **Law 10 – Tree of Thought:** Explore three alternative futures.

8. **Law 11 – Persuasive Prompting:** Convince a skeptic why this matters.

9. **Law 12 – Ethical Prompting:** Consider fairness, harm, and unintended effects.

10. **Law 13 – Reframing:** Present idea in business vs. philosophy lenses.

11. **Law 15 – Industry-Specific Prompts:** Show applications in cybersecurity, education, and healthcare.

12. **Law 17 – Creative Collaboration:** Build ideas together, not apart.

13. **Law 19 – Metaprompting:** Suggest how to improve this very prompt at the end.

Final Task: As the council, generate one groundbreaking, future-proof idea about how humans and AI could co-create a better world - not just a gadget, but a concept that redefines how we live or think.

Sample Output (Demonstration)

Socrates: What if education became dialogue, not lecture every student with a council of minds at their side?

Ada: Designed modularly, it becomes a personal algorithm of learning, adapting as they grow.

Twain: Finally, school would be funny. Imagine Newton explaining gravity with a banana peel.

Sun Tzu: Strategy: arm the next generation not with answers, but with the art of questioning.

Tesla: Delivered wirelessly, of course. A lightning bolt of knowledge into every home.

Dostoevsky: But also a mirror - forcing each learner to face themselves. Without reflection, knowledge is a mask.

Nik (Moderator): Consensus: the **Global Living Curriculum** - timeless minds, AI, and humans co-teaching together. Not static textbooks, but an evolving, witty, ethical dialogue for every learner, everywhere.

Diogenes: And what if governments used such a council - not to dictate laws, but to *stress-test them*? Every new policy facing Socratic questions, Twain's sarcasm, Ada's logic, Sun Tzu's strategy. Perhaps fewer disasters, more wisdom.

177

Nik (Moderator): A **Global Council of Prompts** - where nations test decisions through timeless minds before unleashing them on real citizens. Not rule by AI, but *rule with historic perspective, ethical mirrors, and human judgment amplified.*

Takeaway

The Rosetta Stone Prompt is **not for everyday use.** It is a demonstration, a cathedral, a compass pointing toward the possible.

The lesson: **If you can combine laws deliberately, you can design prompts that don't just answer - they teach, persuade, question, and imagine.**

Or as Twain put it: **"A bad prompt is a fever dream. A good one is a cathedral in miniature."**

For Further Reading:
Explore the full **19 Laws of AI Prompting Intelligence** and more in Nikolay Gul's books here:
Nikolay Gul on Amazon:
https://www.amazon.com/s?k=nikolay+gul

"This is not a daily tool - think of it as a proof-of-concept."

Epilogue – Stepping Out of the Time Machine

We've traveled centuries in a 186 pages - not bad for a roundtable with no seating chart and an AI that occasionally tries to order pizza in Latin.

If these journeys prove anything, it's that prompting is more than words on a screen. It's a way of thinking—framing problems so humans and machines can do their best work together.

The 10 + 1 Laws are a foundation, not a finish line. New models will arrive, tools will tempt, fashions will change. The principles hold: clarity before cleverness; context before output; roles before replies; constraints before creativity; iterate on purpose; teach with analogy; question well; invert the problem; fight bias; anchor ethics; and treat the glitch as a laboratory, not a catastrophe.

A few parting practices to keep you flying level:

- Start every prompt with three lines: **Goal · Audience · Constraints**.

- Run a two-pass review: **Does this say exactly what I mean? → What did it miss?**

- When results wobble, perform a **Prompt Autopsy**: what was missing, misleading, or misordered?

- Add one **Socratic check**: *What am I assuming that might be false?*

- Save your best prompts as **Prompt Cards**. Your future self will thank you.

The Time Machine is always running. You're always welcome back.

Twain: "When in doubt, cut a word—then cut the doubt."
Ada: "Structure first; brilliance follows."
Socrates: "One more question."
Erratta: "Also, for the record, pizza in Latin was a feature, not a bug."

The Time Machine never really stops—it's listening for your next question.

Acknowledgements

The "Permission Granted" Edition

To my wife - for *allowing* me to vanish into the Time Machine for countless hours without sending a search party (or worse, a "to-do" list). Your patience was the real ethical anchor of this entire project.

From the Roundtable:

- **Mark Twain:** "She's clearly the wiser half - any woman who can tolerate a man who talks to dead philosophers and fictional AI deserves a medal... or at least a good vacation."

- **Ada Lovelace:** "Statistical analysis suggests that 97% of successful books were completed only because someone at home looked the other way."

- **Leonardo da Vinci:** "Even my most elaborate machines required less maintenance than a writer in deadline mode. She is the true engineer here."

- **Erratta (AI):** "Calculating probability of you surviving without her support: 0.003%. Rounding down for realism."

- **Nik:** "This book has many laws, but the one that made it possible is The Law of Marital Mercy. Thank you for applying it generously."

To the thinkers, creators, and troublemakers - past, present, and yet to come - who remind us that the best ideas come from unexpected conversations.

To my historical co-conspirators (Ada, Twain, Leonardo, and the rest), whose voices may be fictionalized here but whose wisdom remains timeless.

To the AI models that were patient enough to be part of this experiment, and to the humans who still know when to close the lid on the Time Machine.

And to you, the reader - because without someone curious enough to open this book, it would just be a stack of bound paper with unusually sarcastic footnotes.

About the Author

Nikolay Gul is an author, AI strategist, and entrepreneur known for blending cutting-edge technology with timeless human storytelling. He has published books on AI prompting, cybersecurity, and self-publishing, and is the founder of Future-Proof Marketing Press.

His work has been featured across industries from education to high-tech marketing, always with a signature mix of clarity, wit, and practical insight. When he's not writing, Nikolay is exploring how humor and history can make even the most complex ideas unforgettable.

Visit: linkedin.com/in/webdesignerny/
https://www.amazon.com/s?k=nikolay+gul

Sources & Further Reading

1. Lovelace, Ada. "Notes on the Analytical Engine." (1842)

2. Twain, Mark. "The Wit and Wisdom of Mark Twain."

3. Franklin, Benjamin. "Poor Richard's Almanack."

4. Leonardo da Vinci. "Notebooks." Codex Atlanticus.

5. Bostrom, Nick. "Superintelligence: Paths, Dangers, Strategies." Oxford University Press.

6. Russell, Stuart & Norvig, Peter. "Artificial Intelligence: A Modern Approach."

7. OpenAI – https://openai.com

8. DeepMind – https://deepmind.com

9. Stanford HAI – https://hai.stanford.edu

10. MIT Technology Review – https://www.technologyreview.com

Other Books by Nikolay Gul

AI-Driven Cybersecurity and High-Tech Marketing

ISBN: 979-8-218-61248-1 | ISBN (eBook): 979-8-9927440-0-2 | LCCN: 2025902819

A comprehensive guide to integrating AI into cybersecurity strategies and high-tech marketing, blending real-world case studies with future-proof tactics.

Easy Book Self-Publishing: A Step-by-Step Guide with AI Assistance

ISBN: 979-8-9927440-1-9 | ISBN eBook: 979-8-9927440-2-6 | LCCN: 2025906574

Practical, AI-assisted approach to self-publishing, covering everything from manuscript to marketing with clarity and efficiency.

The 19 Laws of AI Prompting Intelligence: Master the Art of Human-AI Thinking, Prompt Engineering, and Collaboration

ISBN (Paperback): 979-8-9927440-4-0 | ISBN (eBook): 979-8-9927440-3-3 | ISBN (Audiobook): 979-8-9927440-8-8 | LCCN: 2025914398

A practical framework for getting the most out of AI tools, rooted in timeless human communication principles.

AI Time Machine - The Art of Prompting

The Brightest Minds from History Unlock the Secrets to Perfect Prompts with Humor.

ISBN eBook: 979-8-9927440-5-7 | ISBN Paperback: 979-8-9927440-6-4 | ISBN Audiobook: 979-8-9927440-7-1 | LCCN: 2025918179

A practical, humor-laced field manual where Twain, Ada Lovelace, Leonardo, Socrates, and a mischievous AI teach you to turn vague asks into precise, reusable prompts—smart, ethical, and built for both beginners and pros.